MW00720959

Lit Knits

10 Literature-Inspired Knits
by Audry Nicklin

Audry Nicklin Designs

Lit Knits

Designer - Audry Nicklin
Photography - Audry Nicklin; Juliet Nicklin on pgs 4, 16, 18-19, 21, and 95
Tech Editor - Chris Polak
Copy Editor - Alina Sayre
Layout - Audry Nicklin

Dedicated to my long-suffering family.

Copyright © 2013 Audry Nicklin Designs

All rights reserved. No part of this publication may be reproduced in any form or by any means without prior permission of the copyright holders. For personal use only.

ISBN 978-0-9898582-0-5

First Printing

Printed in USA
1984 Printing
Soy-based zero-VOC CMYK inks, 60% PCW recycled paper

www.bear-ears.com/lit-knits

Contents

Introduction

Projects

Resources

Extras

About The Book

Childhood Ambition

When I was really young, I used to spend hours drawing and stapling together little books. In one of my many books, I wrote about all the things I wanted to do when I grew up. One of those things was to be an author.

At some point down the line, I decided I didn't have a novel in me, so the idea of writing a book slowly went away. It didn't occur to me for quite some time that not all books have to be novels.

And So It Began

About two months before beginning this book, I swore I would never write a book. I had only graduated from university a year before and had just left my job at a wool mill. The idea of starting a big project was daunting. Besides, I didn't have a theme in mind.

At about that time, I started to read again. It had taken around a year to recover from all the reading I had done for university. One of the first I picked up was *Anne of Green Gables*. Immediately after finishing it, I was inspired to design a shawl that incorporated bits of the story.

As I worked on getting the pattern released, I ran across an old sketch of mine for a pair of mittens featuring the White Rabbit from *Alice's Adventures in Wonderland*. It seemed like it would be neat to make a collection of literature-themed knits. Then it hit me: I had begun to make a book.

Primary Goals

There were a few goals I had in mind as I worked. Each knit needed to have the story in it. I read each book to ensure that the knits embodied the stories they represented. In many cases I learned that film versions of the books were really toned down. (Tom Sawyer, I'm looking at you.)

While these knits needed to incorporate parts of the books, they couldn't look like costumes. These needed to be knits that could be worn every day. So while "Deep Sea Wanderer" evokes the view through the porthole of the *Nautilus*, it is also a versatile infinity scarf. Even parts of the collection that aren't worn contain subtle nods to the books without looking cartoonish. To the undiscerning eye, "Sail To Treasure Island" looks like a textured blanket with cables. But a closer inspection will reveal a secret: the entire blanket is a map of Treasure Island where X does indeed mark the spot.

Organization

One of the biggest challenges was deciding in what order the knits should be presented. After trying various formats, I decided that the knits should appear in the same order as the publication dates of their respective books. In the case of books published as serials, the day that the full book was published was chosen.

Props And Equipment

To get the right feel in all the photographs, I felt it was important to locate the most authentic props possible. I spent months scouring used bookstores and the internet for old copies of the books. I also had the opportunity to handle some unusual objects. The coin seen on pg 39 is an actual Mexican 8 Reales, also known as a piece of eight. It was borrowed from my Opa's coin collection. The horseshoe seen on pg 33 was found on the wall in a relative's barn.

Further consistency in the photographs was maintained by shooting the entire book with a Canon EOS 60D camera and a 50mm f1.4 lens.

In Closing

To all the knitters out there, I hope you enjoy working on these patterns from your favorite books. Perhaps you will even discover new stories along the way.

-Audry

Tips For Success

Choosing A Size And Considering Ease

Different projects look better with different amounts of ease. All the project measurements in this book are true to size, so in order to get the right fit, it is important to consider how much ease to allow. What exactly is ease? Ease refers to the amount of fabric in relation to a person's final measurement.

For example, someone with a 36"/91cm chest wearing a sweater that measured 35"/89cm would be wearing a sweater that had 1"/2cm of negative ease. The knit would have to stretch, so the sweater would be more form fitting. However, if this individual wore a sweater that was 38"/96cm, they would have 2"/5cm of positive ease. The resulting sweater would hang more loosely around their body.

Some projects need to have a certain amount of ease in order to fit right. Socks and hats often fit better when they have 1"/2.5cm negative ease. Without a little negative ease, socks slide around in shoes and hats are easily shaken off. However, if the project has stranded color work in it, such as "Behind The Garden Wall", it is wiser to choose a size that allows for zero ease, as stranded color work doesn't have much stretch.

Gauge

Making a swatch is invaluable. Without getting the recommended gauge, a project can quickly turn into something that no human could ever hope to wear. I personally have made my fair share of socks that only Sasquatch could fit.

It is important to knit the swatch the same way you are going to knit the finished object. This means that if the project is knit in the round, the swatch should be knit in the round. Many knitters purl more loosely than they knit, so a swatch worked back and forth is not as accurate for a project knit in the round. Swatches for stranded color work projects, such as "Down the Rabbit Hole", need to be done using the color work pattern, since stranded color work has less give than plain stockinette.

How do I make a swatch?
All the projects have a "gauge" section. Cast on the recommended number of stitches, then knit the recommended number of rows. After blocking the swatch and letting it dry, measure it. If the finished measurements match up with the recommended 4x4"/10x10cm, you are ready to start. If you have more stitches and/or rows than recommended, go up in needle size. If you have too few stitches and/or rows, try going down in needle size.

Why do I need to block the swatch?
A swatch must be blocked. Certain fibers, such as superwash wool, often grow when they are washed. An unblocked swatch is often an inaccurate swatch. And while there is forgiveness in the size of a scarf, swatches for projects like sweaters need to be as accurate as possible.

What if I can't get the exact stitch and row gauge?
Unless otherwise noted, it is more important to get stitch gauge than row gauge. In most cases, the project can be made longer or shorter by knitting more or fewer rows.

Blocking

Blocking is where the magic happens in knitting. Even the most experienced knitter's projects can look misshapen without blocking. In the picture below, the two swatches are the same except that the top swatch remains unblocked, while the bottom swatch has been blocked.

How to block
Fill a clean bucket with cool water and pour in some no-rinse wool wash. Let the project soak for 15 minutes. Drain the bucket and gently push the water out of the project. Roll the project up in a towel and pat out the water. Pin the project to the final dimensions with rustproof pins on blocking mats or a flat surface.

A few extra tips
Do not lift the project out of the bucket before the water has been pushed out. The weight of the water will stretch the yarn and distort the project.
Warmer water tends to relax fiber more than cold water, so a project blocked in warm water will often grow more than one blocked in cold water.

Down The Rabbit Hole

Alice's Adventures In Wonderland
Lewis Carroll
1865

"Oh dear! Oh dear! I shall be late!"

Finished Measurements
Small (Large)
10¼"/ 26cm (11¼"/ 28.5cm) cuff to tip;
7"/ 18cm (8"/ 20.5cm) palm to tip;
7"/ 18cm (8¼"/ 21cm) palm
circumference;
2½"/ 6.5cm (3"/ 7.5cm) thumb
circumference

Yarn
Galler Yarns *Prime Alpaca*; 665yds/ 608m
per 8oz/ 227g; 100% Alpaca; sport weight:
1 skein in *Silver Gray* (MC)
1 skein in *Bleached White* (CC)
OR
approx 120 (140)yds/ 110 (128)m (MC),
80 (100)yds/ 73 (92)m (CC) of a sport
weight yarn

Needles/Notions
Size 1 US/ 2.25mm circular needle,
12"/ 30mm or preferred small circular
method
Size 1 US/ 2.25mm set of five double-
point needles
*Change needle size if needed in order to
obtain the correct gauge*
1 stitch marker, waste yarn

Gauge
26sts/ 30rows = 4x4"/ 10x10cm in
Stockinette Stitch
For the most accurate gauge, knit the
swatch using the first 26 stitches of the
first chart

Alice spends what starts out as a boring afternoon along the riverbank with her sister. All of a sudden a white rabbit with a pocketwatch rushes by. What else is a girl to do but follow? Soon she falls down the rabbit hole into another world full of talking animals and strange games. From a paradoxical race where everyone is a winner to a mad tea party, Alice wanders through Wonderland having adventure after adventure.

There have been various theories put forward as to what influenced Lewis Carroll to write *Alice's Adventures in Wonderland*. While many of the images are mind bending, it wasn't until the Jefferson Airplane song "White Rabbit" was released in the 1960s that *Alice's Adventures In Wonderland* started being associated with psychedelic drugs. The story itself started out as a tale to entertain the Liddell children, one of whom was a girl named Alice.

Notes

The color is worked with the stranded method. See the stranded color tutorial on pg 87 for additional help.

Both Mittens

With circular needle, CO 48 (56)sts in MC. Place marker and join in round, taking care not to twist the stitches.

Ribbing Set Up: [K2, p2]
Continue in pattern until work measures 3¼"/ 8.5cm from CO edge.

Size Small ONLY
Next Rnd: [K22, k2tog] twice. 46 sts.

Size Large ONLY
Next Rnd: [K26, k2tog] twice. 54 sts.

Left Mitten

Size Small Mitten ONLY
Work Left Chart - Small: *I Shall Be Late.*
On Rnd 19, knit the first 37 sts as seen on the chart. Knit the next 7 sts with the waste yarn, which is represented as a dark bar on the chart. Slip all waste yarn stitches back onto the left needle and continue knitting in pattern. Waste yarn will later be removed when putting in the thumb.

Size Large Mitten ONLY
Work Left Chart - Large: *I Shall Be Late.*
On Rnd 22, knit the first 44 sts as seen on the chart. Knit the next 9 sts with the waste yarn, which is represented as a dark bar on the chart. Slip all waste yarn stitches back onto the left needle and continue knitting in pattern. Waste yarn will later be removed when putting in the thumb.

All Sizes
Switch to dpns as needed when decreasing at the top of the mitten. Once the chart has been completed, slip the first 9 (13) sts onto one dpn. Slip the remaining 9 (13) sts onto a second dpn. Graft the stitches together in MC.

Insert thumb.

Thumb – Use For Both Mittens

Remove waste yarn and pick up the live stitches with dpns. There will be 7 (9) upper stitches and 7 (9) lower stitches. Pick up an additional stitch between the upper and lower stitches on both sides. 16 (20) sts total. Arrange your dpns so that the first 4 (5) bottom stitches are on the first dpn. The next 3 (4) bottom stitches and the first picked-up stitch is on the second dpn. The first 4 (5) top stitches are on the third dpn and the last 3 (4) top stitches and last picked-up stitch is on the fourth dpn.

Size Small Mitten ONLY
For both left and right mitten, work Thumb Chart - *Small* beginning with the first dpn.
Continue in pattern until the thumb measures 2½"/ 6.5cm or reaches desired length.

With MC, [Ssk, k4, k2tog] twice.

Slip the first 6 sts onto one dpn. Slip the remaining 6 sts onto a second dpn. Graft the thumb together with MC.

Size Large Mitten ONLY
For the left mitten, work Left Thumb Chart - *Large* beginning with the first dpn.
For the right mitten, work Right Thumb Chart - *Large* beginning with the first dpn.
Continue in pattern until the thumb measures 2½"/ 6.5cm or reaches desired length.

With MC, [Ssk, k6, k2tog] twice.

Slip the first 8 sts onto one dpn. Slip the remaining 8 sts onto a second dpn. Graft the thumb together with MC.

Right Mitten

Size Small Mitten ONLY
Work Right Chart - Small: *Down The Rabbit Hole.*
On Rnd 19, knit the first 2 sts as seen on the chart. Knit the next 7 sts with the waste yarn, which is represented as a dark bar on the chart. Slip all waste yarn stitches back onto the left needle and continue knitting in pattern. Waste yarn will later be removed when putting in the thumb.

Size Large Mitten ONLY
Work Right Chart - Large: *Down The Rabbit Hole.*
On Rnd 22, knit the first 1 st as seen on the chart. Knit the next 9 sts with the waste yarn, which is represented as a dark bar on the chart. Slip all waste yarn stitches back onto the left needle and continue knitting in pattern. Waste yarn will later be removed when putting in the thumb.

All Sizes
Switch to dpns as needed when decreasing at the top of the mitten. Once the chart has been completed, slip the first 9 (13) sts onto one dpn. Slip the remaining 9 (13) sts onto a second dpn. Graft the stitches together in MC.

Insert thumb.

Finishing

Weave in all ends and block both mittens. After the mittens are blocked, the clock hands will be sewn onto the left mitten.

Sewing The Clock Hands

Using the MC, cut a length of 24"/ 61cm. Fold the yarn in half and sew on the clock hands as seen on the diagram below.

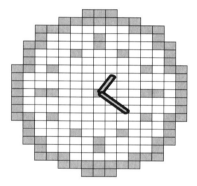

The time on the chart is 1:22, but any time can be sewn into the clock. Just be sure that both clock hands start on the center grey stitch. Once the clock hands are secure, weave in the ends.

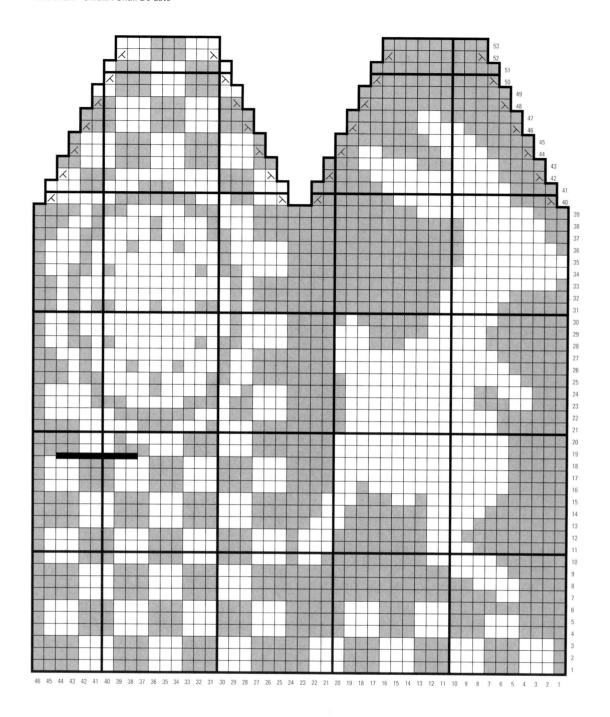

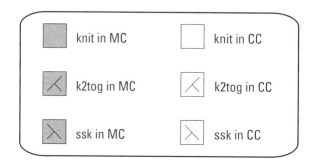

Right Chart - Small: *Down The Rabbit Hole*

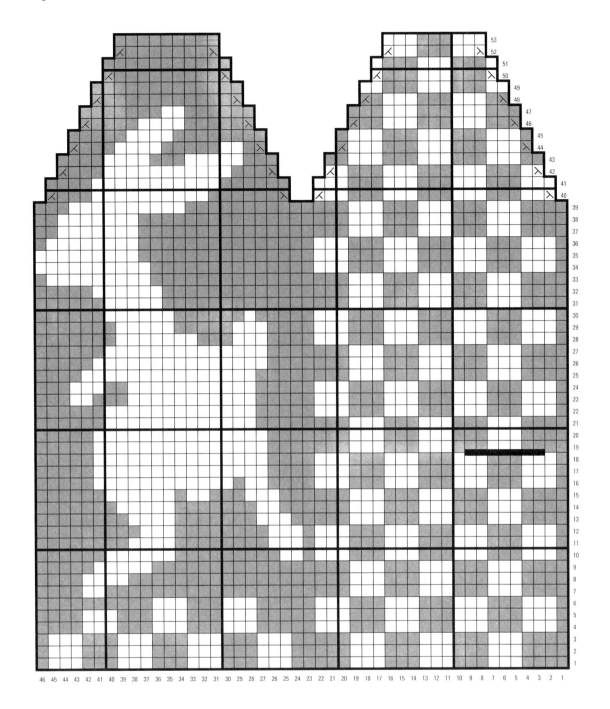

Thumb Chart - *Small*

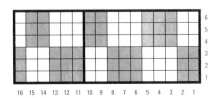

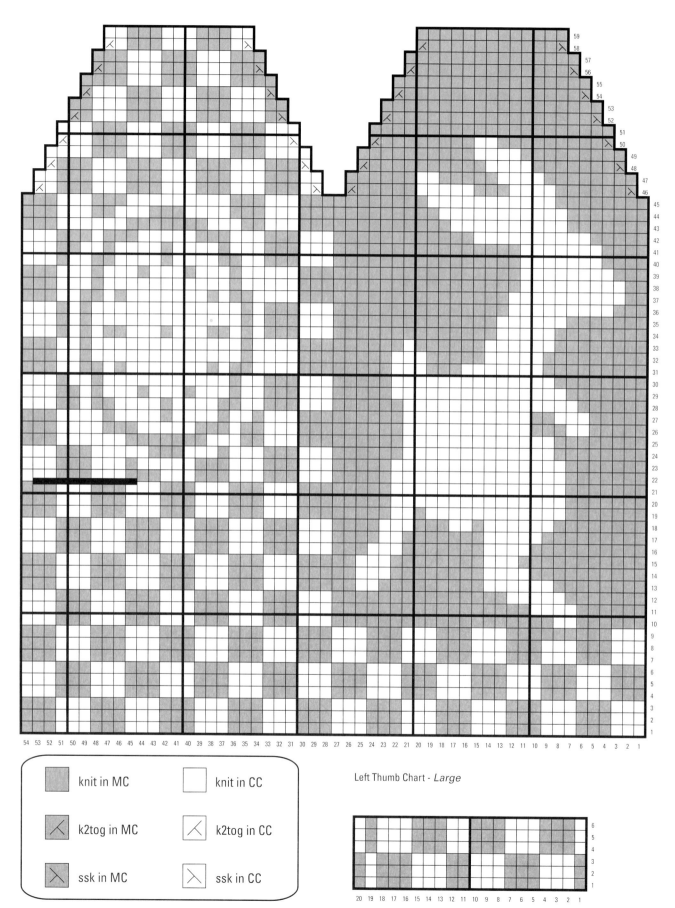

Left Thumb Chart - *Large*

knit in MC	knit in CC
k2tog in MC	k2tog in CC
ssk in MC	ssk in CC

Right Chart - Large: *Down The Rabbit Hole*

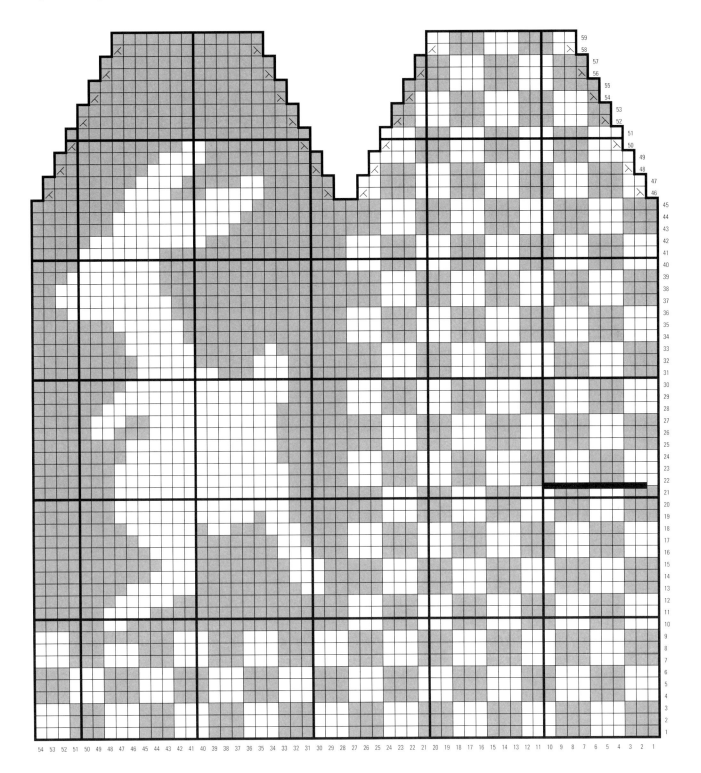

Right Thumb Chart - *Large*

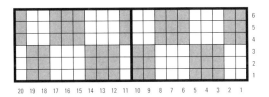

Brinker

Hans Brinker or The Silver Skates
Mary Mapes Dodge
1865

"A cloud of feathery ice flies from the heels of the skaters as they 'bring to' and turn at the flag staffs."

Chapter XLIV: The Race

Finished Measurements
Medium (Large)
18¾"/ 48cm (22½"/ 57cm) circumference;
10"/ 25cm deep with brim rolled down;
8"/ 20cm deep with brim rolled up

Yarn
Malabrigo Yarn *Merino Worsted*; 210yds/
192m per 3.5oz/ 100g skein; 100% Merino
Wool; aran weight:
1 skein in #27 *Bobby Blue* (MC)
1 skein in #63 *Natural* (CC)
OR
approx 150yds/ 137m (MC),
100yds/ 91m (CC) of an aran weight yarn

Needles/Notions
Size 8 US/ 5.0mm circular needle,
16"/ 40cm or preferred small circular
method
Size 8 US/ 5.0mm set of five double-point
needles
*Change needle size if needed in order to
obtain the correct gauge*
Cable needle, 1 stitch marker

Gauge
16sts/ 24rows = 4x4"/ 10x10cm in
Stockinette Stitch

Hans Brinker and his sister Gretel live a humble life in Holland. Their father is left disabled after an accident at work, so the rest of the family pulls together to make a living.

During the winter, all children skate along the frozen waterways. A skating race is organized and the top prize is a pair of silver skates. Although poor, Hans is industrious and carves himself and his sister a pair of wooden skates each. Unlike steel skates that cut into the ice and allow for good traction, wooden skates can only glide on top of the ice. The brother and sister are excellent skaters, but stand little to no chance of winning the race without good steel skates. However, once the siblings set their minds to something, very little can stop them.

Brim

CO 75 (90) sts with the CC. Place marker and join in round, taking care not to twist the stitches.

Ribbing Set Up: [K1, p2]
Continue in established ribbing pattern until work measures 2"/ 5cm from CO edge.

With CC, work rnds 1-4 of Chart 1: *Skaters To Your Mark.* Switch to MC on rnd 5. Work rnds 5-16 of Chart 1: *Skaters To Your Mark* once through, then work Chart 1: *Skaters To Your Mark* once more, ending on rnd 15. Do not work rnd 16 a second time.

Work Chart 2: *Race To The Finish* once through.
45 (54)sts will remain after completing Chart 2: *Race To The Finish.*

Crown Shaping

Change to dpns as needed while shaping crown.

Rnd 1: [K2tog, k2, k2tog, k3]
Rnd 2: [K1, k2tog, k2, k2tog]
Rnd 3: [K2tog, k1, k2tog] 15sts (18sts).

Size Large: 22½"/ 57cm ONLY
Next Rnd: [K2tog] (9sts).

Finishing

Cut the yarn, thread it through the remaining stitches, and cinch together. Weave in all the ends and block.
Make a pom-pom and attach to the top of the hat. See pom-pom tutorial on pg 92 for additional help.

Chart 1: *Skaters To Your Mark*

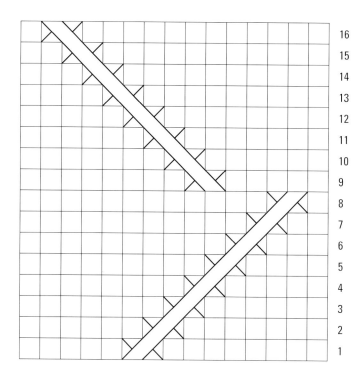

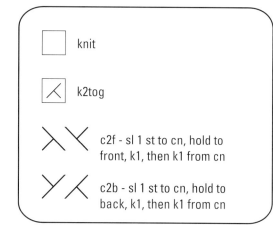

knit

k2tog

c2f - sl 1 st to cn, hold to front, k1, then k1 from cn

c2b - sl 1 st to cn, hold to back, k1, then k1 from cn

Chart 2: *Race To The Finish*

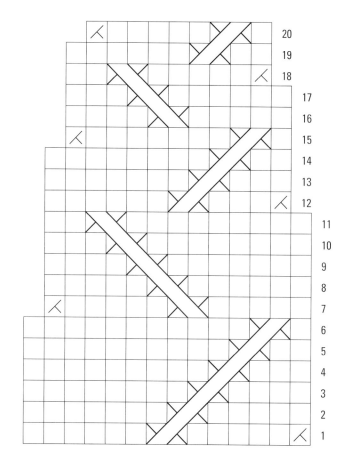

Written Instructions

c2f - sl 1 sts to cn, hold to front, k1, then k1 from cn
c2b - sl 1 sts to cn, hold to back, k1, then k1 from cn

Chart 1: *Skaters To Your Mark*
Rnd 1: [K8, C2B, k5]
Rnd 2: [K7, C2B, k6]
Rnd 3: [K6, C2B, k7]
Rnd 4: [K5, C2B, k8]
Rnd 5: [K4, C2B, k9]
Rnd 6: [K3, C2B, k10]
Rnd 7: [K2, C2B, k11]
Rnd 8: [K1, C2B, k12]
Rnd 9: [K5, C2F, k8]
Rnd 10: [K6, C2F, k7]
Rnd 11: [K7, C2F, k6]
Rnd 12: [K8, C2F, k5]
Rnd 13: [K9, C2F, k4]
Rnd 14: [K10, C2F, k3]
Rnd 15: [K11, C2F, k2]
Rnd 16: [K12, C2F, k1]

Chart 2: *Race To The Finish*
Rnd 1: [K2tog, k5, C2B, k6]
Rnd 2: [K5, C2B, k7]
Rnd 3: [K4, C2B, k8]
Rnd 4: [K3, C2B, k9]
Rnd 5: [K2, C2B, k10]
Rnd 6: [K1, C2B, k11]
Rnd 7: [K5, C2F, k5, k2tog]
Rnd 8: [K6, C2F, k5]
Rnd 9: [K7, C2F, k4]
Rnd 10: [K8, C2F, k3]
Rnd 11: [K9, C2F, k2]
Rnd 12: [K2tog, k3, C2B, k6]
Rnd 13: [K3, C2B, k7]
Rnd 14: [K2, C2B, k8]
Rnd 15: [K1, C2B, k7, k2tog]
Rnd 16: [K5, C2F, k4]
Rnd 17: [K6, C2F, k3]
Rnd 18: [K2tog, k5, C2F, k2]
Rnd 19: [K2, C2B, k6]
Rnd 20: [K1, C2B, k5, k2tog]

Crown Shaping
Rnd 1: [K2tog, k2, k2tog, k3]
Rnd 2: [K1, k2tog, k2, k2tog]
Rnd 3: [K2tog, k1, k2tog] 15sts (18sts)

Size Large: 22½"/ 57cm ONLY
Next Rnd: [K2tog] (9sts)

Deep Sea Wanderer

20,000 Leagues Under The Sea
Jules Verne
1870

"Such was the region our *Nautilus* was visiting just then: a genuine prairie, a tightly woven carpet of algae, gulfweed, and bladder wrack so dense and compact a craft's stempost couldn't tear through it without difficulty."

Chapter XI: Sargasso Sea

Finished Measurements
55"/ 140cm circumference;
6½"/16.5cm height

Yarn
Madelinetosh *Tosh DK*; 225yds/ 206m
per 3.5oz/ 100g; 100% Superwash Merino
Wool; dk weight: 2 skeins in *Cousteau*
OR
approx 450yds/ 412m of a dk weight yarn

Needles/Notions
Size 5 US/ 3.75mm circular needle,
32"/ 80cm
*Change needle size if needed in order to
obtain the correct gauge*
1 stitch marker

Gauge
20sts/ 28rows = 4x4"/ 10x10cm in
Stockinette Stitch

After being captured by Captain Nemo, famous marine biologist Professor Pierre Aronnax finds pleasure in sitting by a window of the *Nautilus*. He passes the time witnessing the wonders that lie below the ocean. Beyond the rivets of the porthole, Aronnax sees odd creatures, forests of seaweed, and rare treasures.

Over the course of the journey, Professor Aronnax travels a distance of 20,000 leagues underneath the water. Never does the *Nautilus* go 20,000 leagues deep. To go straight down 20,000 leagues would result in going through the earth and coming out about a fifth of the way to the moon on the other side.

Infinity Scarf

CO 216 sts loosely. Place marker and join in round, taking
care not to twist the stitches.
Work Chart 1: *Lower Porthole Riveting* once though.
Work Chart 2: *Sargasso Seaweed* three times through, then
rounds 1 and 2 once more.
Work Chart 3: *Upper Porthole Riveting* once through.
BO all stitches loosely. Weave in ends and block.

Chart 1: *Lower Portal Riveting*

Chart 3: *Upper Portal Riveting*

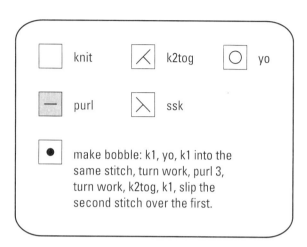

knit

k2tog

yo

purl

ssk

make bobble: k1, yo, k1 into the same stitch, turn work, purl 3, turn work, k2tog, k1, slip the second stitch over the first.

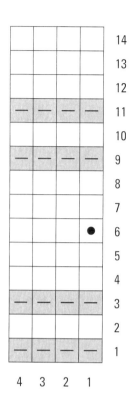

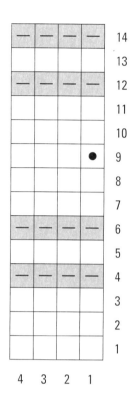

Chart 2: *Sargasso Seaweed*

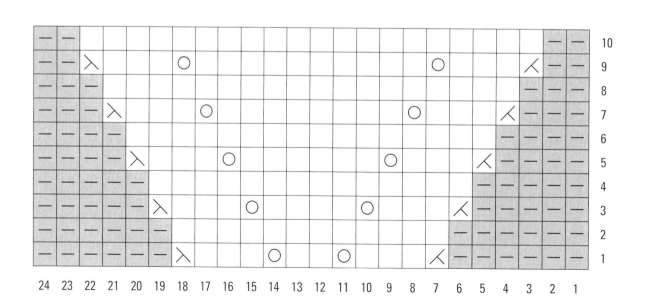

Written Instructions

Make bobble: k1, yo, k1 into the same stitch, turn work, purl 3, turn work, k2tog, k1, slip the second stitch over the first.

Chart 1: *Lower Porthole Riveting*
Rnd 1: Purl
Rnd 2: Knit
Rnd 3: Purl
Rnds 4-5: Knit
Rnd 6: [Make bobble, k3]
Rnd 7-8: Knit
Rnd 9: Purl
Rnd 10: Knit
Rnd 11: Purl
Rnds 12-14: Knit

Chart 2: *Sargasso Seaweed*
Rnd 1: [P6, k2tog, k3, yo, k2, yo, k3, ssk, p6]
Rnd 2: [P6, k12, p6]
Rnd 3: [P5, k2tog, k3, yo, k4, yo, k3, ssk, p5]
Rnd 4: [P5, k14, p5]
Rnd 5: [P4, k2tog, k3, yo, k6, yo, k3, ssk, p4]
Rnd 6: [P4, k16, p4]
Rnd 7: [P3, k2tog, k3, yo, k8, yo, k3, ssk, p3]
Rnd 8: [P3, k18, p3]
Rnd 9: [P2, k2tog, k3, yo, k10, yo, k3, ssk, p2]
Rnd 10: [P2, k20, p2]

Chart 3: *Upper Porthole Riveting*
Rnds 1-3: Knit
Rnd 4: Purl
Rnd 5: Knit
Rnd 6: Purl
Rnds 7-8: Knit
Rnd 9: [Make bobble, k3]
Rnds 10-11: Knit
Rnd 12: Purl
Rnd 13: Knit
Rnd 4: Purl

Tomfoolery

The Adventures of Tom Sawyer
Mark Twain
1876

"Like it? Well, I don't see why I oughtn't to like it. Does a boy get a chance to whitewash a fence every day?"

Chapter II: The Glorious Whitewasher

Finished Measurements
4"/ 10cm width;
84"/ 213cm length

Yarn
O-Wool *Balance*; 130yds/ 119m per 1.75oz/ 50g; 50% Merino Wool, 50% Cotton; dk weight:
2 skeins in #1000 *Natural* (MC)
1 skein in #8014 *Agate* (CC)
OR
approx 260yds/ 199m (MC), 40 yds/ 36.5m (CC) of a dk weight yarn

Needles/Notions
Size 5 US/ 3.75mm needles
Change needle size if needed in order to obtain the correct gauge

Gauge
26sts/ 20rows = 4x4"/ 10x10cm in [k2, p2] ribbing, stretched

Tom Sawyer never has to look for trouble. Trouble always finds him. On occasion, Tom's misbehaviors catch up with him and his Aunt Polly assigns a punishment, the most famous being the chore of whitewashing her fence. Of course Tom convinces all his friends that nothing could be more fun than whitewashing. He acts as if no one else should even be allowed to join in, which only tantalizes his friends more. Before long, they are bribing Tom for the privilege of painting his aunt's fence. By the end, the nine-foot-high, thirty-yard-long fence has three coats of whitewash on it.

The whitewash Tom used was probably made of a simple mixture of chalk, water, and calcium hydroxide. Once applied, it would take a period of days to harden.

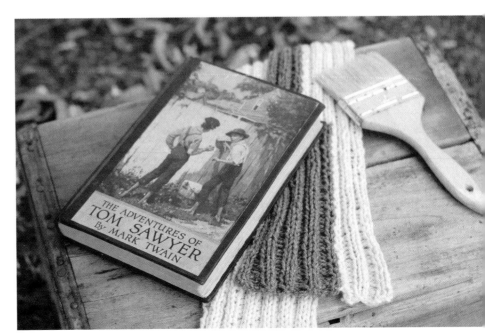

Notes

The color is worked with the intarsia method. See the intarsia tutorial on pg 87 for additional help.

Scarf

CO 17sts with CC and 9sts with MC.

Next row (RS): With MC, [K2, p2] two times, k1. Switch to CC. K1, [p2, k2] four times.

Next row (WS): With CC, [P2, k2] four times, p1. Switch to MC. P1, [k2, p2] two times.

Continue knitting in pattern until the scarf measures 7"/18cm from cast on edge, ending with a WS row. Break the CC.

Next row (RS): With the MC, [k2, p2] four times, k1. Rejoin CC and k1, [p2, k2] two times.

Next row (WS): With CC, [P2, k2] two times, p1. With MC, p1, [k2, p2] four times.

Continue knitting in pattern until the scarf measures 11"/28cm from the cast on edge, ending with a WS row. Break the CC.

Next row (RS): With MC, [K2, p2] until last two stitches. Knit remaining stitches.

Next row (WS): [P2, k2] until last two stitches. Purl remaining stitches.

Continue in pattern until the scarf measures 84"/ 213cm or reaches the desired length.

BO in pattern and weave in all the ends. Block the scarf.

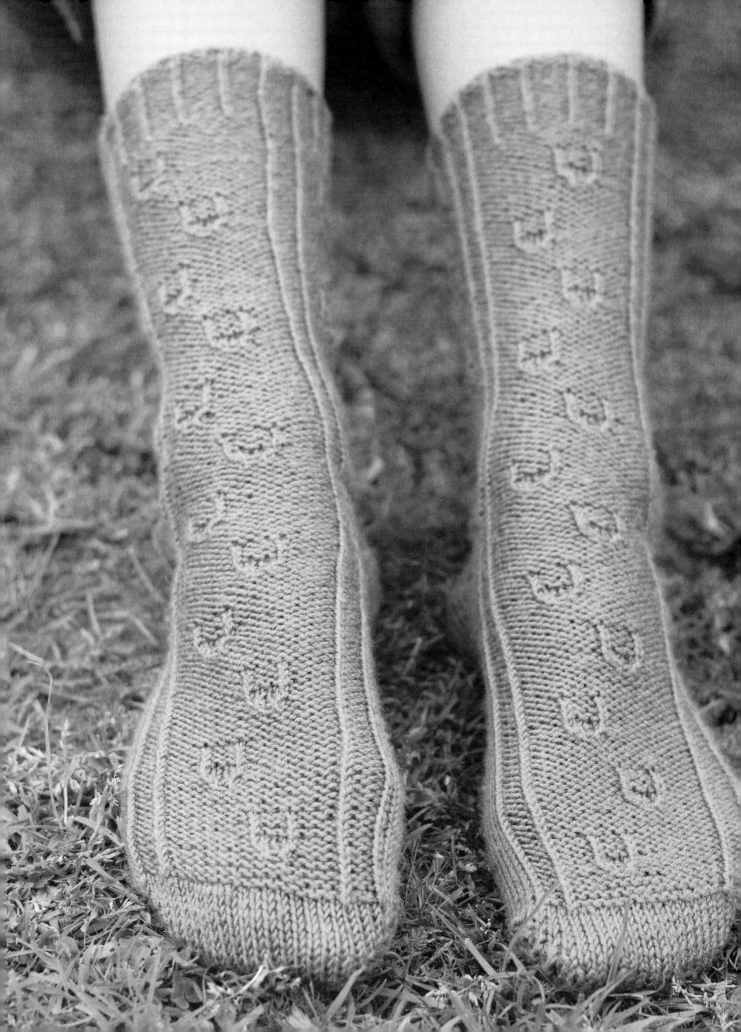

Black Beauty Rides On

Black Beauty
Anna Sewell
1877

"It was a great treat to us to be turned out into the home paddock or the old orchard; the grass was so cool and soft to our feet, the air so sweet, and the freedom to do as we liked was so pleasant—to gallop, to lie down, and roll over on our backs, or to nibble the sweet grass."

Chapter VI: Liberty

Finished Measurements
X-Small (Small, Medium, Large);
7½ (8¼, 9, 10)"/ 19 (21, 23, 25.5)cm around calf and ball of foot unstretched;
7¼"/ 18.5cm from top of heel to top of cuff

Yarn
Frog Tree *Pediboo*; 255 yds/ 233m per 3.5oz/ 100g; 80% Merino Wool/ 20% Bamboo; fingering weight: 2 (2, 2, 2) skeins in #1110 *Grey*
OR
approx 300 (350, 380, 420)yds/ 275 (320, 348, 384)m of a fingering weight yarn

Needles/Notions
Size 0 US/ 2.0mm circular needle, 12"/ 30mm or preferred small circular method
Change needle size if needed in order to obtain the correct gauge
Size B/ 2.25mm hood for provisional CO
Cable needle, 2 stitch markers, waste yarn

Gauge
29sts/ 40rows = 4x4"/ 10x10cm in Stockinette Stitch

Black Beauty is born belonging to a well-off gentleman. Although he is a wonderful horse, Black Beauty has an accident and throws a shoe. Horse hooves are strong, but when a horse is worked, ridden, or kept in a damp climate, horseshoes are necessary to protect the hoof from wear and breakage. Black Beauty's foot is damaged and he stumbles and falls, scarring his knees.

In a world where image means everything to the affluent, Beauty, no longer flawless, is sold. However, he remains positive even in the midst of hardships, and eventually finds his reward.

Short Row Toe

With waste yarn, CO 27 (30, 33, 36) provisional stitches. See pg 85 for provisional cast on tutorial for additional help.

Knit across the provisional stitches. Turn the work and purl to the last stitch, then w&t. Knit to the last stitch, then w&t. Purl to the stitch before the wrap, then w&t. Continue until there are 6 (7, 8, 9) wraps on each side. There will be 15 (16, 17, 18) unwrapped stitches in between.
Purl to the first wrap, pick up the wrap, then w&t the next stitch. That stitch will be double wrapped. Continue picking up wraps, then w&t. Pick up double wraps as you get to them. See pg 93 for short row tutorial for additional help.

Once the short row toe is complete, unravel the provisional cast on. Pick up the live stitches and knit across. 54 (60, 66, 72) sts.

Next Rnd: [K27 (31, 33, 37), pm, k26 (28, 32, 34), pm]. Do not knit the last stitch in the round. The second placed marker indicates the beginning of the round. The first 28 (32, 34, 38) sts are the top of the foot and the remaining 26 (28, 32, 34) sts are the bottom of the foot.

Left Foot ONLY
Rnd 1: Knit rnd 1 of Chart 1: *Hoofing It*, sm, knit to end.

Right Foot ONLY
Rnd 1: Knit rnd 11 of Chart 1: *Hoofing It*, sm, knit to end.

Both Socks
Next Rnd: Work next rnd of Chart 1: *Hoofing It*, sm, knit to end.
Once the entire 20 rnds of the chart has been completed, begin again at rnd 1.
Continue in pattern until sock measures 2"/ 5cm from total desired foot length.

Short Row Heel

Knit the top 28 (32, 34, 38) sts in pattern, sm, begin short row heel. The short row heel is made the same way the short row toe was. There will be 14 (14, 16, 16) sts in between wraps and 6 (7, 8, 9) wraps on each side. To complete the heel, pick up wraps in the same manner as the toe until all wraps have been picked up.

Leg

Next Rnd: Work next rnd of Chart 1: *Hoofing It*, sm, knit to end.

Continue in pattern until either round 10 or 20 of Chart 1: *Hoofing It* has been completed.

Set Up Rnd: Remove the stitch marker indicating the beginning of the round. K3 (3, 2, 2), k1 tbl, p1 (2, 3, 4). Replace the marker. This is now the beginning of the round. Chart 2: *The Long Haul* will start here.

Switch to Chart 2: *The Long Haul*. If round 10 of Chart 1: *Hoofing It* was worked last, then round 11 of Chart 2: *The Long Haul* will be worked next. If round 20 of Chart 1: *Hoofing It* was worked last, then round 1 of Chart 2: *The Long Haul* will be worked next Chart 2: *The Long Haul* will be worked three times around the entire sock.

Next Rnd: Work Chart 2: *The Long Haul*. Remove the second stitch marker when it is reached.

Continue in pattern until three full repeats of Chart 2: *The Long Haul* have been completed, ending on round 4 or 14.

Cuff

54 and 72 stitch sock cuff ONLY
[P1, k1 tbl, p1]

60 stitch sock cuff ONLY
[P2, k1 tbl *p2, k1 tbl* 5 times, p2]

66 stitch sock cuff ONLY
[P3, k1 tbl *p2, k1 tbl* 5 times, p3]

Continue in pattern until cuff measures 1½"/ 3.5cm long.

Finishing

BO loosely in established pattern. Use a knit stitch rather than k1 tbl while binding off. Make the second sock with the pattern mirrored to the first. The left sock begins with rnd 1 of Chart 1: *Hoofing It* and the right sock begins with rnd 11 of Chart 1: *Hoofing It*.
Weave in all ends and block.

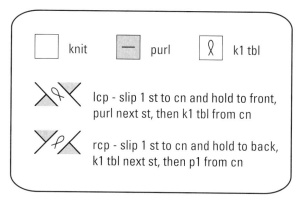

| | knit | | — | purl | | 𝚈 | k1 tbl |

lcp - slip 1 st to cn and hold to front, purl next st, then k1 tbl from cn

rcp - slip 1 st to cn and hold to back, k1 tbl next st, then p1 from cn

Chart 1: *Hoofing It*   Work blue boxed area 3 (3, 2, 2) times total
Work black boxed area 1 (2, 3, 4) time(s) total

Chart 2: *The Long Haul*   Work black boxed area
1 (2, 3, 4) time(s) total

Written Instructions

rcp - slip 1 to cn and hold to back, k1 tbl next stitch, then p1 from cn
lcp - slip 1 to cn and hold to front, purl next stitch, then k1 tbl from cn

Chart 1: *Hoofing It*
Rnds 1-4: K3 (3, 2, 2), k1 tbl, p2 (4, 6, 8), k1 tbl, p14, k1 tbl, p2 (4, 6, 8), k1 tbl, k3 (3, 2, 2), sm, k26 (28, 32, 34)
Rnd 5: K3 (3, 2, 2), k1 tbl, p2 (4, 6, 8), k1 tbl, p8, k1 tbl, k1 tbl, p4, k1 tbl, p2 (4, 6, 8), k1 tbl, k3 (3, 2, 2), sm, k26 (28, 32, 34)
Rnd 6: K3 (3, 2, 2), k1 tbl, p2 (4, 6, 8), k1 tbl, p7, rcp, lcp, p3, k1 tbl, p2 (4, 6, 8), k1 tbl, k3 (3, 2, 2), sm, k26 (28, 32, 34)
Rnd 7: K3 (3, 2, 2), k1 tbl, p2 (4, 6, 8), k1 tbl, p7, k1 tbl, k2, ktbl, p3, k1 tbl, p2 (4, 6, 8), k1 tbl, k3 (3, 2, 2), sm, k26 (28, 32, 34)
Rnds 8-10: K3 (3, 2, 2), k1 tbl, p2 (4, 6, 8), k1 tbl, p7, k1 tbl, p2, ktbl, p3, k1 tbl, p2 (4, 6, 8), k1 tbl, k3 (3, 2, 2), sm, k26 (28, 32, 34)
Rnds 11-14: K3 (3, 2, 2), k1 tbl, p2 (4, 6, 8), k1 tbl, p14, k1 tbl, p2 (4, 6, 8), k1 tbl, k3 (3, 2, 2), sm, k26 (28, 32, 34)
Rnd 15: K3 (3, 2, 2), k1 tbl, p2 (4, 6, 8), k1 tbl, p4, k1 tbl, k1 tbl, p8, k1 tbl, p2 (4, 6, 8), k1 tbl, k3 (3, 2, 2), sm, k26 (28, 32, 34)
Rnd 16: K3 (3, 2, 2), k1 tbl, p2 (4, 6, 8), k1 tbl, p3, rcp, lcp, p7, k1 tbl, p2 (4, 6, 8), k1 tbl, k3 (3, 2, 2), sm, k26 (28, 32, 34)
Rnd 17: K3 (3, 2, 2), k1 tbl, p2 (4, 6, 8), k1 tbl, p3, k1 tbl, k2, k1 tbl, p7, k1 tbl, p2 (4, 6, 8), k1 tbl, k3 (3, 2, 2), sm, k26 (28, 32, 34)
Rnds 18-20: K3 (3, 2, 2), k1 tbl, p2 (4, 6, 8), k1 tbl, p3, k1 tbl, p2, k1 tbl, p7, k1 tbl, p2 (4, 6, 8), k1 tbl, k3 (3, 2, 2), sm, k26 (28, 32, 34)

Chart 2: *The Long Haul*
Rnds 1-4: [P1 (2, 3, 4), k1 tbl, p14, k1 tbl, p1 (2,3,4)]
Rnd 5: [P1 (2, 3, 4), k1 tbl, p8, k1 tbl, k1 tbl, p4, k1 tbl, p1 (2,3,4)]
Rnd 6: [P1 (2, 3, 4), k1 tbl, p7, rcp, lcp, p3, k1 tbl, p1 (2,3,4)]
Rnd 7: [P1 (2, 3, 4), k1 tbl, p7, k1 tbl, k2, k1 tbl, p3, k1 tbl, p1(2,3,4)]
Rnds 8-10: [P1 (2, 3, 4), k1 tbl, p7, k1 tbl, p2, k1 tbl, p3, k1 tbl, p1(2,3,4)]
Rnds 11-14: [P1 (2, 3, 4), k1 tbl, p14, k1 tbl, p1(2,3,4)]
Rnd 15: [P1 (2, 3, 4), k1 tbl, p4, k1 tbl, ktbl, p8, k1 tbl, p1(2,3,4)]
Rnd 16: [P1 (2, 3, 4), k1 tbl, p3, rcp, lcp, p7, k1 tbl, p1(2,3,4)]
Rnd 17: [P1 (2, 3, 4), k1 tbl, p3, k1 tbl, k2, k1 tbl, p7, k1 tbl, p1(2,3,4)]
Rnds 18-20: [P1 (2, 3, 4), k1 tbl, p3, k1 tbl, p2, k1 tbl, p7, k1 tbl, p1(2,3,4)]

Sail To Treasure Island

Treasure Island
Robert Louis Stevenson
1883

"The doctor opened the seals with great care, and there fell out the map of an island, with latitude and longitude, soundings, names of hills and bays and inlets, and every particular that would be needed to bring a ship to a safe anchorage upon its shores."

Chapter VI: The Captain's Papers

Finished Measurements
62" x 62"/ 157cm x 157cm

Yarn
Cascade Yarns *128 Superwash*; 128 yds/ 117m per 3.5oz/ 100g; 100% Superwash Merino Wool; bulky weight: 17 skeins in #1926 *Doeskin Heather*
OR
approx 2176yds/ 1990m of a bulky weight yarn

Needles/Notions
Size 10 US/ 6.0mm set of five double-point needles
Size 10 US/ 6.0mm circular needle, 16"/ 40cm; 24"/ 60cm; 40"/ 100cm
2 Size 10 US/ 6.0mm circular needles, 60"/ 150cm
Change needle size if needed in order to obtain the correct gauge
8 stitch markers

Gauge
14sts/ 21rows = 4x4"/ 10x10cm in Stockinette Stitch

Jim Hawkins hosts Billy Bones at the Admiral Benbow Inn. Bones served under the fearsome pirate, Captain Flint. But even more feared than the captain is the quartermaster, Long John Silver.

A quartermaster on a pirate ship ranked just below the captain and held great sway in making decisions for the ship. Yet despite his power, Silver still needs a map to find Flint's treasure.

Pirates come looking for Bones and the map, but Jim beats them to it. He eventually finds himself befriending a one-legged cook upon the *Hispaniola* and sailing to Treasure Island.

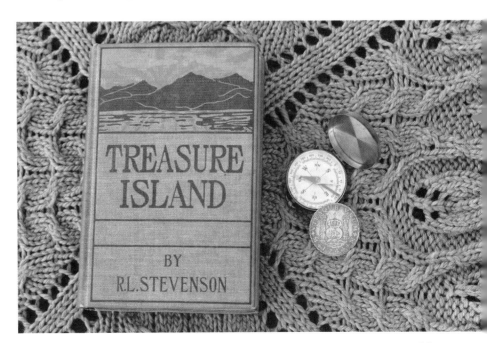

Notes

All the charts represent a quarter of the blanket. Each chart should be knit four times through to complete the round.

The blanket is knitted from the center out. As stitch numbers increase, switch to longer circular needles as needed. When the 60"/ 150cm circular needles become too short, knit the first half of the stitches with the first 60"/ 150cm circular needle and the second half of the stitches on the second 60"/ 150cm circular needle.

Cast On

With dpns, CO 4 sts using the circular cast on. See pg 86 for circular cast on tutorial for additional help. Place a marker when joining in round to indicate the beginning of the round.

Rnd 1: Knit
Rnd 2: [M1L, k1] 8 sts.
Rnd 3: Knit
Rnd 4: [M1L, k2] 12 sts.
Rnd 5: Knit
Rnd 6: [M1L, k2, m1R, k1] 20 sts.
Rnd 7: Knit
Rnd 8: [yo, k2, yo, pm, k3, pm] 28 sts.
Rnd 9: [K4, sm, k3, sm]

Work Chart 1: *Shadow Of Spy-Glass Hill*
176 sts at the end of rnd 43.

Work Chart 2: *Lofty Groves*
312 sts at the end of rnd 51.

Work Chart 3: *Buried Among The Trees*
384 sts at the end of rnd 67.

Work Chart 4: *Melancholy Woods*
456 sts at the end of rnd 75.

Work Chart 5: *Sodden Leaves*
528 sts at the end of rnd 84.

Work Chart 6: *Marshy Tract*
384 sts at the end of rnd 93.

Work Chart 7: *High Water Mark*
396 sts at the end of rnd 100.

Work Chart 8: *Sandy Shores*
468 sts at the end of rnd 118.

Work Chart 9: *Ocean Swells* once through, then repeat rnds 119-139 once more.

For a larger blanket, continue repeating Chart 9 until the blanket reaches the desired size. Be sure to purchase extra yarn to accommodate the larger blanket.

BO loosely. Weave in all ends and block.

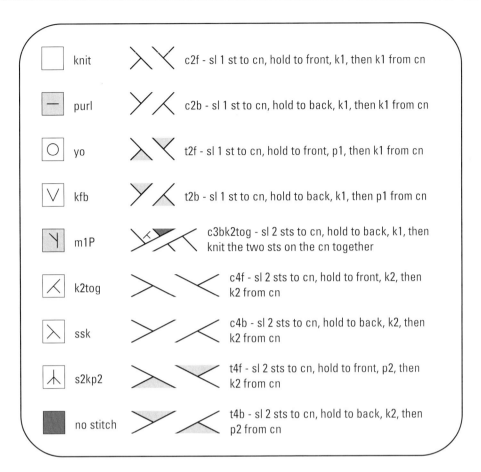

knit	$\diagdown\diagup$	c2f - sl 1 st to cn, hold to front, k1, then k1 from cn
purl	$\diagup\diagdown$	c2b - sl 1 st to cn, hold to back, k1, then k1 from cn
O yo	$\diagdown\diagdown$	t2f - sl 1 st to cn, hold to front, p1, then k1 from cn
V kfb	$\diagup\diagdown$	t2b - sl 1 st to cn, hold to back, k1, then p1 from cn
Y m1P		c3bk2tog - sl 2 sts to cn, hold to back, k1, then knit the two sts on the cn together
K k2tog		c4f - sl 2 sts to cn, hold to front, k2, then k2 from cn
ssk		c4b - sl 2 sts to cn, hold to back, k2, then k2 from cn
s2kp2		t4f - sl 2 sts to cn, hold to front, p2, then k2 from cn
no stitch		t4b - sl 2 sts to cn, hold to back, k2, then p2 from cn

Chart 1: *Shadow Of Spy-Glass Hill*   Work boxed area 2 times total

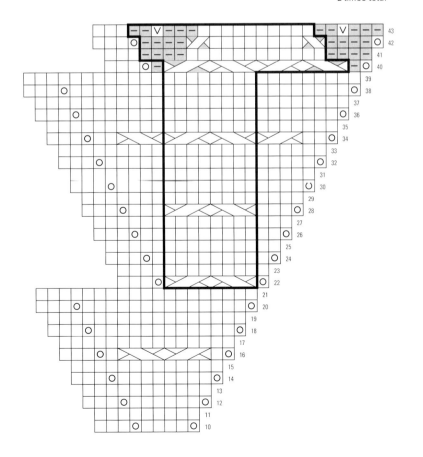

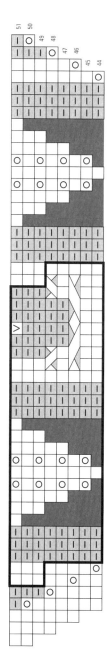

Chart 2: *Lofty Groves*   Work boxed area 2 times total

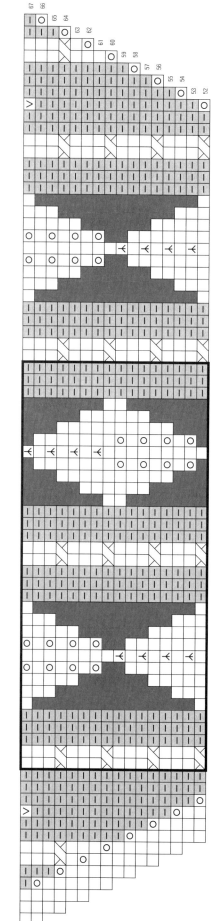

Chart 3: *Buried Among The Trees*   Work boxed area 2 times total

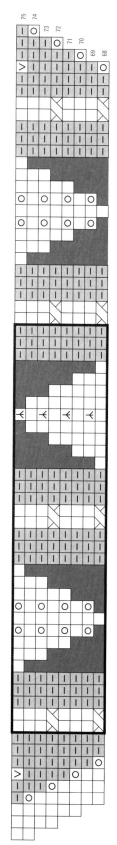

Chart 4: *Melancholy Woods*   Work boxed area 3 times total

Chart 5: *Sodden Leaves*   Work boxed area 4 times total

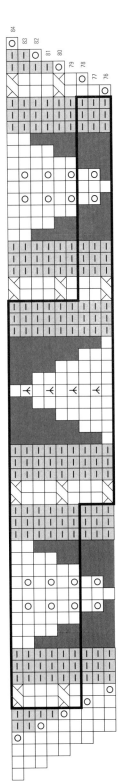

Chart 6: *Marshy Tract*   Work black boxed area 4 times total
Work blue boxed area 5 times total

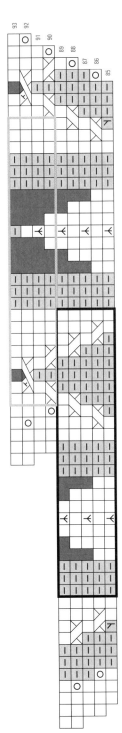

Chart 8: *Sandy Shores*   Work boxed area 12 times total

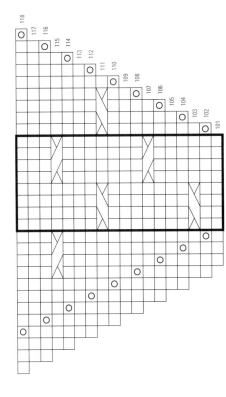

Chart 7: *High Water Mark*   Work boxed area 5 times total

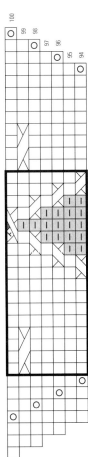
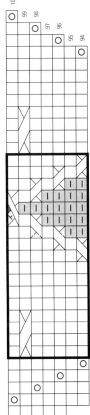

Chart 9: *Ocean Swells*

Work boxed area 7 times total the first time through
Work boxed area 8 times total the second time through

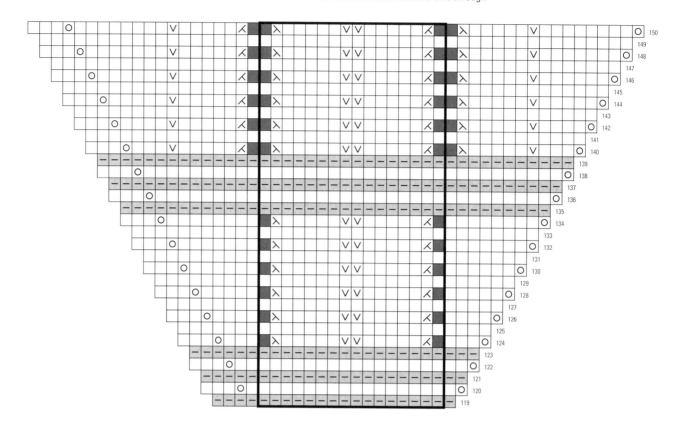

Robin Hoodie

The Merry Adventures Of Robin Hood
Howard Pyle
1883

"Then Robin took his good yew bow in his hand, and placing the tip at his instep, he strung it right deftly; then he nocked a broad clothyard arrow and, raising the bow, drew the gray goose feather to his ear; the next moment the bowstring rang and the arrow sped down the glade as a sparrowhawk skims in a northern wind."

Chapter I: How Robin Hood Came To Be An Outlaw

Finished Measurements
Sizes: Allan a Dale (Will Scarlet, Robin Hood, Will Stutely, Friar Tuck, Little John)
Chest circumference: 36 (40, 44, 48, 52, 56)"/ 91 (102, 112, 122, 132, 142)cm

2-4"/ 5-10cm of positive ease is recommended. The model has a 37"/ 94cm chest and is wearing size 40"/ 102cm.

Yarn
Brooklyn Tweed *Shelter*; 140yds/ 128m per 1.76oz/ 50g; 100% Wool; worsted weight: 8 (9, 10, 11, 12, 13) skeins in *Tent*
OR
approx 1110 (1230, 1350, 1510, 1650, 1770) yds/ 1015 (1125, 1235, 1380, 1510, 1620)m of a worsted weight yarn

Needles/Notions
Size 7 US/ 4.5mm circular needle, 16"/ 40cm or preferred small circular method; 32"/ 80cm
Change needle size if needed in order to obtain the correct gauge
Size G/ 4.0mm hook for provisional CO
Cable needle, 5 stitch markers, waste yarn

Gauge
16sts/ 26rows = 4x4"/10x10 cm using Chart 2: *Sherwood Forest*

After killing one of the king's deer and a man, Robin Hood retreats to Sherwood Forest as an outlaw. Over time men join him becoming known as the merry men. Among them are Allan a Dale, a bard; Will Scarlet, Robin's cousin; Will Stutely, who is often left in charge; Friar Tuck, the group's chaplain, and Little John, Robin's close friend who bested him in a fight of quarterstaves.

Lincoln green, which was dyed with the plants woad and weld, was the color of choice for clothing among the merry men.

Notes

This sweater is knit from the top down, starting at the hood. The hood is worked flat and has cabling on both sides. Once the hood is complete, the sweater is joined at the neck and worked in the round.

Hood

All Sizes

Use a provisional cast-on to CO 96 sts. Leave a 24"/ 61cm tail for grafting the hood together later. See pg 85 for provisional cast on tutorial for additional help.

Work Chart 1: *Shades Of The Greenwood*.
Chart is repeated four times across each row.
Work Chart 2: *Sherwood Forest* six times for a total of 98 rows from the CO edge. The hood will measure approx 15"/ 38cm from the CO edge.

Yoke

Work Chart 3: *Merry Men*.
Work each row of the chart twice through to complete each round.
Rnd 1: Knit the first 17 sts of the chart, pm, knit the next 18 sts of the chart, pm, knit the next 34 sts of the chart. Keep in mind that after the last 17 sts on the chart have been knit, the chart will be repeated. Pm, knit the next 18sts of the chart, pm, knit the remaining 17 sts of the chart, pm. This is now the beginning of the round.
Rnd 2: Join the round. Continue in pattern.

For a lower neckline, continue working Chart 3: *Merry Men* flat. Join in round when the desired neckline has been achieved.

Complete Chart 3: *Merry Men*.
240 sts at the end of round 36.

Sweater Body

Size 36: Allan a Dale ONLY
Separate the Arms from the body:
*Following round 1 of Chart 4 - Size 36: *Allan a Dale*, knit to the first marker. Remove the marker, slip the next 52 sleeve stitches onto waste yarn. Remove the second marker. Use a backwards loop or provisional cast on to CO 4 sts. Knit in pattern to the next marker. Repeat from * once more. Keeping in pattern, knit the remaining stitches. 144 body stitches.
Starting on rnd 2, work the rest of Chart 4 - Size 36: *Allan a Dale*.

Work Chart 2: *Sherwood Forest* starting on round 6. Chart is repeated 6 times across each row.

Continue knitting the sweater body in pattern using Chart 2: *Sherwood Forest* until the body reaches approximately 14"/ 35.5cm or 3"/7.5cm less than desired length from the underarm. End on round 8 of the Chart 2: *Sherwood Forest*.

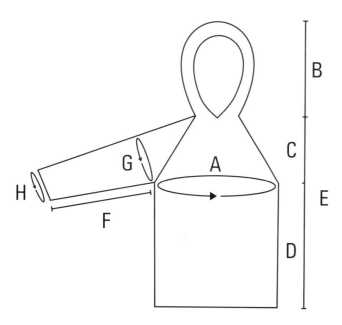

A - Chest/ Hip Circumference: 36 (40, 44, 48, 52, 56)"/ 91 (102, 112, 122, 132, 142)cm
B - Hood: All Sizes 15"/ 38cm
C - Yoke: 5 ½ (6¾ , 7¾ , 9, 10¼ , 11)"/ 14 (17, 19.5, 23, 26, 28)cm
D - Body: All Sizes 17"/ 43cm
E - Full Length: 22 ½ (23¾, 24¾, 26, 27¼, 28)"/ 57 (60.5, 63, 66, 69, 71)cm
F - Sleeve Length: All Sizes 18"/ 46cm
G - Upper Arm Circumference: 14 (16, 18, 20, 22, 24)"/ 35.5 (40.5, 45.5, 51, 56, 61)
H - Cuff Circumference: 12 (12, 12, 14, 14, 14)" / 30 (30, 30, 35, 35, 35)cm

Note on Pattern Repeats for Size 40: Will Scarlet and Size 44: Robin Hood ONLY

When working the body with Chart 2: *Sherwood Forest*, a repeat and a half of the pattern will be worked before reaching the first marker (i.e. sts 1-24, then 1-12). Knit plain to the second marker. Between the second and third marker, three full repeats of the Chart 2: *Sherwood Forest* will be worked to the third marker, starting on stitch 13 and ending on stitch 12 (i.e. 13-24, 1-24 twice, 1-12). Knit plain to the fourth marker. From the fourth marker to the end of the round, another repeat and a half of the pattern will be worked, starting on stitch 13 (i.e. 13-24, 1-24).

Size 40: Will Scarlet ONLY
Work rounds 1-8 of the Chart 4 - Sizes 40, 44: *Robin Hood*. 272 sts.
Separate the arms from the body:
*Following round 9 of Chart 5 - Size 40: *Will Scarlet*, knit to the first marker. Remove the marker, slip the next 60 sleeve stitches onto waste yarn. Remove the second marker. Use a backwards loop or provisional cast on to CO 4 sts. Knit in pattern to the next marker. Repeat from * once more. Keeping in pattern, knit the remaining stitches. 160 body stitches.
Work rounds 10 and 11 of Chart 5 - Size 40: *Will Scarlet*.

Work Chart 2: *Sherwood Forest* starting on round 6. Knit the first 36 sts in pattern, pm, knit the next 8 sts, pm, knit the next 72 sts in pattern, pm, knit the next 8 sts, pm, knit the remaining 36 sts in pattern.

See *Note on Pattern Repeats for Size 40: Will Scarlet and Size 44: Robin Hood* for additional help on how to work the repeats of Chart 2: *Sherwood Forest* around the body.

Continue knitting the sweater body in pattern using Chart 2: *Sherwood Forest* until the body reaches approximately 14"/ 35.5cm or 3"/ 7.5cm less than desired length from the underarm. End on round 8 of the Chart 2: *Sherwood Forest*.

Size 44: Robin Hood ONLY
Work rounds 1-14 of Chart 4 - Sizes 40, 44: *Robin Hood*. 296 sts.
Separate the arms from the body:
*Following round 15 of the Chart 4 - Sizes 40, 44: *Robin Hood*, knit to the first marker. Remove the marker, slip the next 66 sleeve stitches onto waste yarn. Remove the second marker. Use a backwards loop or provisional cast on to CO 6 sts. Knit in pattern to the next marker. Repeat from * once more. Keeping in pattern, knit the remaining stitches. 176 body stitches.

Work Chart 2: *Sherwood Forest* starting on round 10. Knit the first 36 sts in pattern, pm, knit the next 16 sts, pm, knit the next 72 sts in pattern, pm, knit the next 16 sts, pm, knit the remaining 36 sts in pattern.

See *Note on Pattern Repeats for Size 40: Will Scarlet and Size 44: Robin Hood* for additional help on how to work the repeats of Chart 2: *Sherwood Forest* around the body.

Continue knitting the sweater body in pattern using Chart 2: *Sherwood Forest* until the body reaches approximately 14"/ 35.5cm or 3"/ 7.5cm less than desired length from the underarm. End on round 8 of the Chart 2: *Sherwood Forest*.

Size 48: Will Stutely ONLY

Work rounds 1-22 of Chart 4: Sizes 48, 52, 56: *Little John*. 328 sts.

Separate the arms from the body:

*Following round 23 of the Chart 5 - Size 48: *Will Stutely*, knit to the first marker. Remove the marker, slip the next 74 sleeve stitches onto waste yarn. Remove the second marker. Use a backwards loop or provisional cast on to CO 6 sts. Knit in pattern to the next marker. Repeat from * once more. Keeping in pattern, knit the remaining stitches. 192 body stitches.

Work rounds 24-26 of Chart 5 - Size 48: *Will Stutely*.

Work Chart 2: *Sherwood Forest* starting on round 6. Chart is repeated 8 times across each row.

Continue knitting the sweater body in pattern using Chart 2: *Sherwood Forest* until the body reaches approximately 14"/ 35.5cm or 3"/ 7.5cm less than desired length from the underarm. End on round 8 of the Chart 2: *Sherwood Forest*.

Size 52: Friar Tuck ONLY

Work rounds 1-30 of Chart 4: Sizes 48, 52, 56: *Little John*. 360 sts.

Separate the arms from the body:

*Following round 31 of Chart 5 - Size 52: *Friar Tuck*, knit to the first marker. Remove the marker, slip the next 82 sleeve stitches onto waste yarn. Remove the second marker. Use a backwards loop or provisional cast on to CO 6 sts. Knit in pattern to the next marker. Repeat from * once more. Keeping in pattern, knit the remaining stitches. 208 body stitches.

Work Chart 2: *Sherwood Forest* starting on round 12. Knit the first 48 sts in pattern, pm, knit the next 8 sts, pm, knit the next 96 sts in pattern, pm, knit the next 8 sts, pm, knit the remaining 48 sts in pattern.

Continue knitting the sweater body in pattern using Chart 2: *Sherwood Forest* until the body reaches approximately 14"/ 35.5cm or 3"/ 7.5cm less than desired length from the underarm. End on round 8 of the Chart 2: *Sherwood Forest*.

Size 56: Little John ONLY

Work rounds 1-36 of Chart 4: Sizes 48, 52, 56: *Little John*. 384 sts.

Separate the arms from the body:

*Following round 37 of Chart 4: Sizes 48, 52, 56: *Little John*, knit to the first marker. Remove the marker, slip the next 88 sleeve stitches onto waste yarn. Remove the second marker. Use a backwards loop or provisional cast on to CO 8 sts. Knit in pattern to the next marker. Repeat from * once more. Keeping in pattern, knit the remaining stitches. 224 body stitches.

Work Chart 2: *Sherwood Forest* starting on round 4. Knit the first 48 sts of the sweater body in pattern, pm, knit the next 16 sts, pm, knit the next 96 sts in pattern, pm, knit the next 16 sts, pm, knit the remaining 48 sts in pattern.

Continue knitting the sweater body in pattern using Chart 2: *Sherwood Forest* until the body reaches approximately 14"/ 35.5cm or 3"/ 7.5cm less than desired length from the underarm. End on round 8 of the Chart 2: *Sherwood Forest*.

Sweater Hem

All Sizes
Work Chart 6: *Hidden In The Undergrowth* in place of the Chart 2: *Sherwood Forest*.

> **Note on Pattern Repeats for Size 40: Will Scarlet and Size 44: Robin Hood ONLY**
> Stitch repeats will be worked in the same fashion as the Chart 2: *Sherwood Forest*.

Next Rnd (Ribbing Set Up): [p1, k2, p1]
Continue in Ribbing pattern for 2"/ 5cm or until desired length has been reached.

BO loosely in pattern.

Sleeve

With the 16"/ 40cm circular needle or preferred small circular method, remove the waste yarn and pick up 2 (6, 9, 13, 17, 20) sts, pm, pick up the next 48 sts, pm, pick up the remaining 2 (6, 9, 13, 17, 20) sts.
Rejoin yarn. Pick up and knit the 4 (4, 6, 6, 6, 8) underarm CO stiches. Place a marker in the center of the CO stitches. This marks the beginning of the round.

Knit to first marker, sm, work Chart 2: *Sherwood Forest*, starting with round 9 (3, 9, 3, 11, 3) to the next marker, sm, knit to end of round. 56 (64, 72, 80, 88, 96) sleeve sts.

Work sleeve for 1"/ 2.5cm.

Next Rnd (Dec Rnd): K2tog, work to first marker, sm, work in pattern, sm, knit to last 2 sts of the round, ssk.

Work a decrease round every 4½ (2, 1¼, 1¼, 1, ¾)"/ 11.5 (5, 3, 3, 2.5, 2)cm until 48 (48, 48, 56, 56, 56) sleeve stitches remain.

Sizes 36, 40, and 44 ONLY
During the last decrease round, all stitch markers except the beginning of the round marker will be removed. The first and last stitches in the chart will be used to complete the last decreases.

Once all the decrease rounds have been completed, continue in pattern using Chart 2: *Sherwood Forest* until the sleeve reaches approximately 15"/ 38 cm or 3"/ 7.5cm less than desired length from the underarm. End on round 8 of the Chart 2: *Sherwood Forest*. Knit rounds 1-5 of the Chart 6: *Hidden In The Undergrowth* in place of the Chart 2: *Sherwood Forest*.

Next Rnd (Ribbing Set Up): [p1, k2, p1]
Continue in Ribbing pattern for 2"/ 5cm or until desired length has been reached.
BO loosely in pattern.

Make the second sleeve the same as the first.

Finishing

Weave in all the ends except at the top of the hood. Block the sweater. Graft the top of the hood together. See grafting tutorial on pgs 88-90 for additional help.

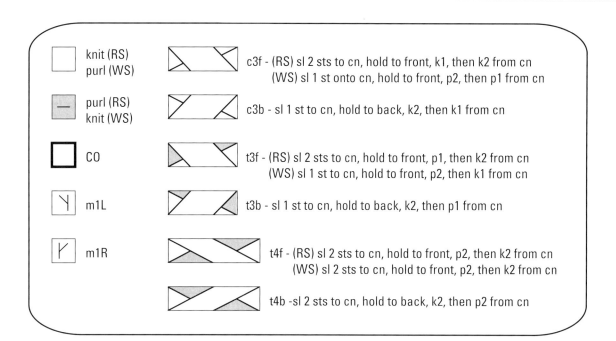

knit (RS)
purl (WS)

purl (RS)
knit (WS)

CO

m1L

m1R

c3f - (RS) sl 2 sts to cn, hold to front, k1, then k2 from cn
(WS) sl 1 st onto cn, hold to front, p2, then p1 from cn

c3b - sl 1 st to cn, hold to back, k2, then k1 from cn

t3f - (RS) sl 2 sts to cn, hold to front, p1, then k2 from cn
(WS) sl 1 st to cn, hold to front, p2, then k1 from cn

t3b - sl 1 st to cn, hold to back, k2, then p1 from cn

t4f - (RS) sl 2 sts to cn, hold to front, p2, then k2 from cn
(WS) sl 2 sts to cn, hold to front, p2, then k2 from cn

t4b -sl 2 sts to cn, hold to back, k2, then p2 from cn

Chart 1: *Shades Of The Greenwood*

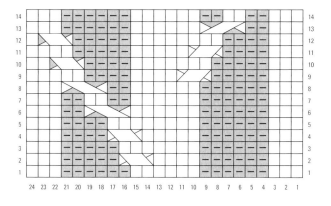

Chart 2: *Sherwood Forest*

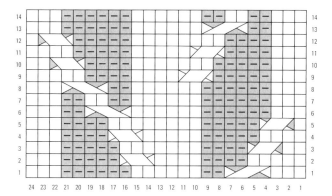

Working Chart 3: *Merry Men*
The chart has been split in half. Both halves must be used in order to work a full row, i.e. Work Row 1 on Chart 3: *Merry Men*, then Row 1 on Chart 3: *Merry Men* (cont'd).
In order to make the knitting easier, make a copy of the page, cut the two halves apart and tape them together with the sleeve portion of each chart meeting.

Chart 3: *Merry Men*

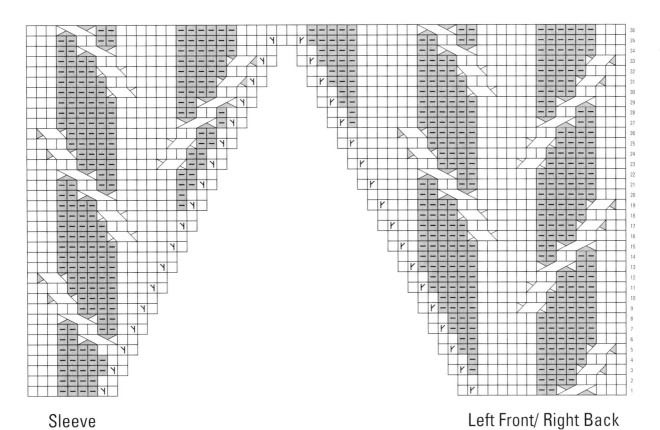

Sleeve

Left Front/ Right Back

Chart 3: *Merry Men* (cont'd)

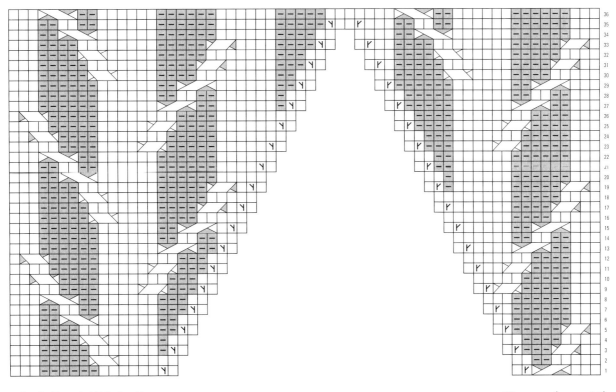

Left Back/ Right Front

Sleeve (cont'd)

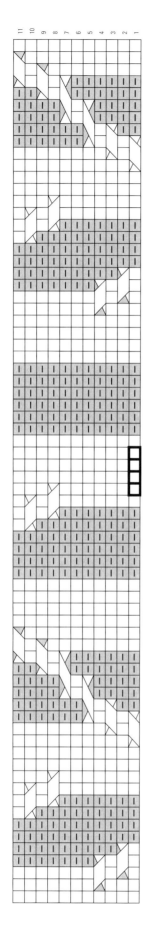

Chart 4 - Size 36: *Allan a Dale*

Working Chart 5 - Size 40: *Will Scarlet*
The chart has been split in half. Both halves must be used in order to work a full row, i.e. Work Row 9 on Chart 5 - Size 40: *Will Scarlet*, then Row 9 on Chart 5 - Size 40: *Will Scarlet* (cont'd).

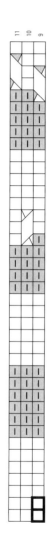

Chart 5 - Size 40: *Will Scarlet*

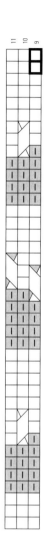

Chart 5 - Size 40: *Will Scarlet* (cont'd)

Chart 4 - Sizes 40, 44: *Robin Hood*

Work blue boxed area 2 times total

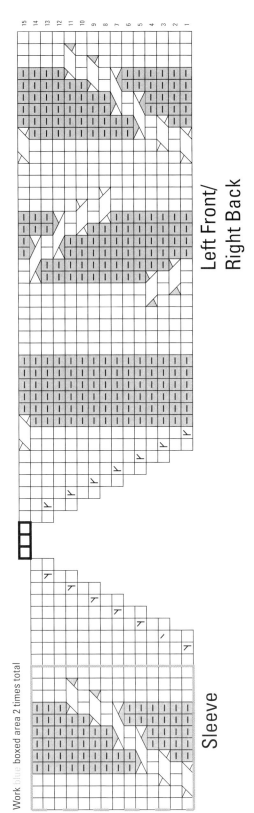

Left Front/
Right Back

Chart 4 - Sizes 40, 44: *Robin Hood* (cont'd)

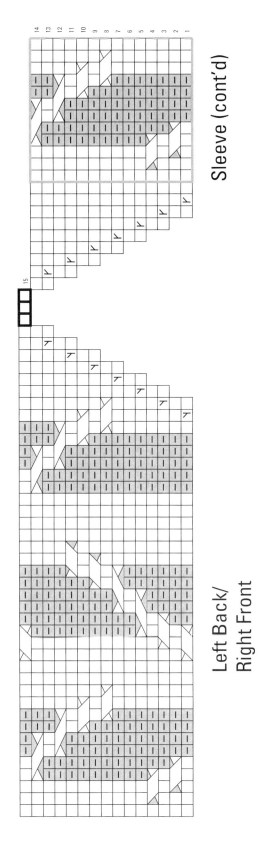

Sleeve

Left Back/
Right Front

Sleeve (cont'd)

Working Chart 4 - Sizes 40, 44: *Robin Hood*

The chart has been split in half. Both halves must be used in order to work a full row, i.e. Work Row 1 on Chart 4 - Sizes 40, 44: *Robin Hood*, then Row 1 on Chart 4 - Sizes 40, 44: *Robin Hood* (cont'd).

The sleeve portion of the chart is also split in half. There is a dotted blue line indicating how the charts join together. In order to make the knitting easier, make a copy of the page, cut the two halves apart and tape them together with the sleeve portion of each chart meeting.

Chart 4 - Sizes 48, 52, 56: *Little John*

Work blue boxed area 2 times total total

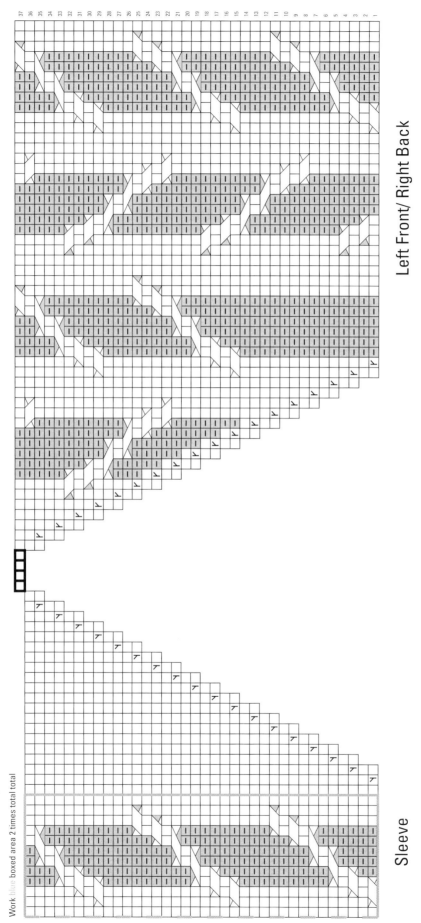

Left Front/ Right Back

Sleeve

Working Chart 4 - Sizes 48, 52, 56: *Little John*

The chart has been split in half between two pages. Both pages must be used in order to work a full row, i.e. Work Row 1 on Chart 4 - Sizes 48, 52, 56: *Little John*, then Row 1 on Chart 4 - Sizes 48, 52, 56: *Little John* (cont'd).
The sleeve portion of the chart is also split in half. There is a dotted blue line indicating how the charts join together.
In order to make the knitting easier, make a copy of both pages and tape them together with the sleeve portion of each chart meeting.

Chart 4 - Sizes 48, 52, 56: *Little John* (cont'd)

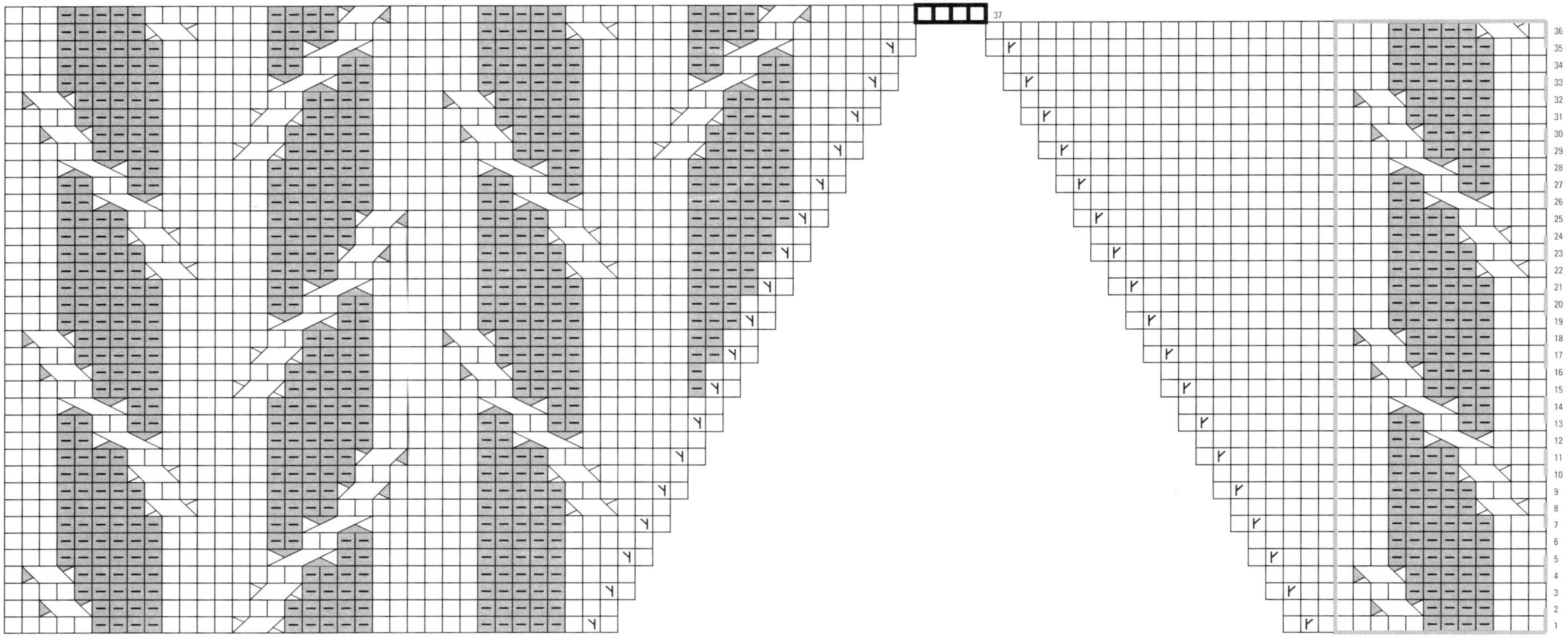

Sleeve (cont'd)

Left Back/ Right Front

Working Chart 5 - Size 48: *Will Stutely*
The chart has been split in half. Both halves must be used in order to work a full row, i.e. Work Row 23 on Chart 5 - Size 48: *Will Stutely*, then Row 23 on Chart 5 - Size 48: *Will Stutely* (cont'd).

Chart 5 - Size 48: *Will Stutely*

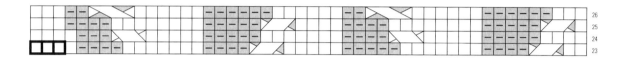

Chart 5 - Size 48: *Will Stutely* (cont'd)

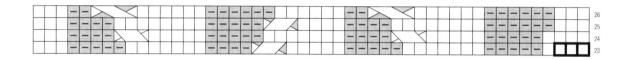

Chart 5 - Size 52: *Friar Tuck*   Work blue boxed areas each 2 times total

Chart 6: *Hidden In The Undergrowth*

Avonlea

Anne Of Green Gables
L.M. Montgomery
1908

"But it's a million times nicer to be Anne of Green Gables than Anne of nowhere in particular, isn't it?"

Chapter VIII: Anne's Bringing-Up Is Begun

Finished Measurements
52"/ 132cm along the top edge;
30½"/ 77.5cm from center back to
bottom tip

Yarn
O-Wool *Classic 2-Ply*; 198yds/ 181m per
1.75oz/ 50g; 100% Certified Organic Merino Wool; fingering weight: 3 skeins in
#3014 *Sage*
OR
approx 550yds/ 503m of a fingering
weight yarn

Needles/Notions
Size 4 US/ 3.5mm circular needle,
32"/ 80cm
*Change needle size if needed in order to
obtain the correct gauge*
4 stitch markers

Gauge
18sts/ 36rows = 4x4"/ 10x10cm in
Stockinette Stitch

Orphaned young, Anne Shirley finds herself living in many families and orphanages. Eventually she is adopted by the Cuthberts who live on Prince Edward Island. This island is a Canadian province that was named for Queen Victoria's father: Prince Edward, Duke of Kent and Strathearn. There is a bit of a mix-up though: the Cuthberts mean to adopt a boy who can work the farm. Instead they get Anne, a little girl with an enormous imagination.

As Matthew and Anne ride from the train station to the town of Avonlea, Anne starts renaming all the places they pass. The Avenue becomes The White Way of Delight, and Barry's Pond becomes The Lake of Shining Waters. But Green Gables needs no new name. It feels like home just as soon as Anne sees it.

Notes

Charts 1-5 are not mirrored. Work them the same way on the left and right side of the shawl. The garter stitch edging is not shown on the charts.
Chart 6 is mirrored. Both sides are shown for convenience. Because of the increases along the garter stitch edging shifts, the edging is shown in the charts.

CO 3 sts. Knit 6 rows. Do not turn work. Rotate the piece 90 degrees clockwise. Pick up and knit 3 sts. (The stitches are in the garter stitch ridge.) Rotate the piece 90 degrees clockwise again. Pick up and knit 3 sts on the end of the tab. 9 sts.
See the tab cast on tutorial on pg 85 for additional help.

Set up Row (WS): K3, p3, k3

Row 1 (RS): K3, pm, m1L, k1, m1R, pm, k1, pm, m1L, k1, m1R, pm, k3. 13 sts.

From row 2 to 142, the first and last three stitches will be knit on every row.

Row 2 (WS): K3, sm, purl to marker, sm, p1, sm, purl to marker, sm, k3.
Row 3 (RS): K3, sm, m1L, knit to marker, m1R, sm, k1, sm, m1L, knit to marker, m1R, sm, k3.
Rows 4-42 even: Repeat row 2.
Rows 5-41 odd: Repeat row 3.
93 sts at the end of row 42.

Work Chart 1: *Green Gables.*
145 sts at the end of row 67.

Work Chart 2: *Garden Fence.*
161 sts at the end of row 76.

Work Chart 3: *Background Flowers.*
185 sts at the end of row 88.

Work Chart 4: *Midground Flowers.*
233 sts at the end of row 112.

Work Chart 5: *Foreground Flowers.*
289 sts at the end of row 140.

Work Chart 6: *Lake of Shining Waters.*
301 sts at the end of row 151.

Rows 152-153: Knit

BO all stitches. Weave in ends and block.

To get defined points in the Lake of Shining Waters and the Green Gables portions of the shawl, refer to the dots on the shawl schematic.

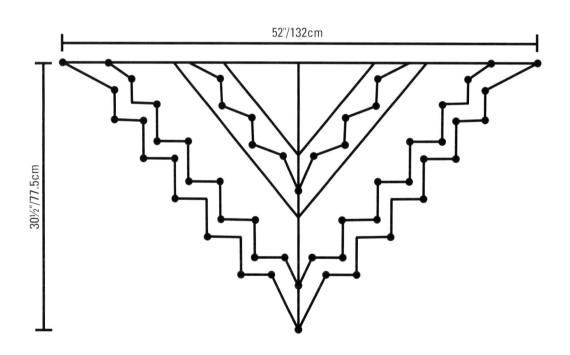

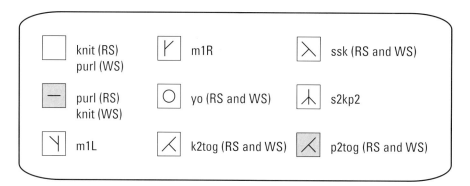

Chart 1: *Green Gables*   Work boxed area 2 times total

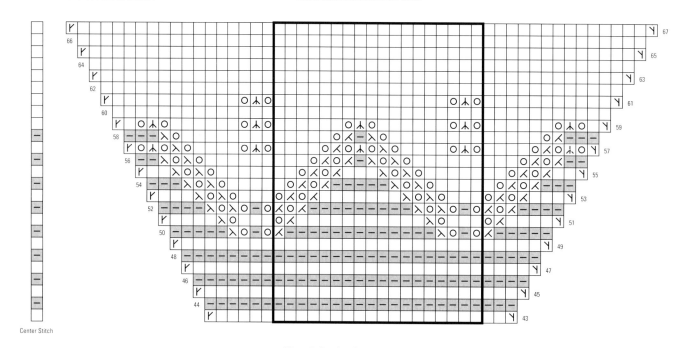

Center Stitch

Chart 2: *Garden Fence*
Work boxed area 33 times total

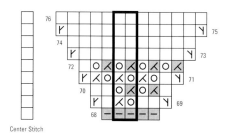

Center Stitch

Chart 3: *Background Flowers*   Work boxed area 6 times total

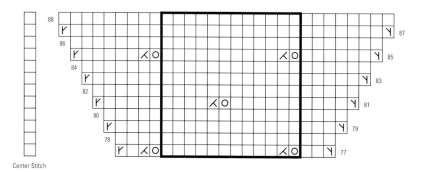

Center Stitch

Chart 4: *Midground Flowers*

Work boxed area 7 times total

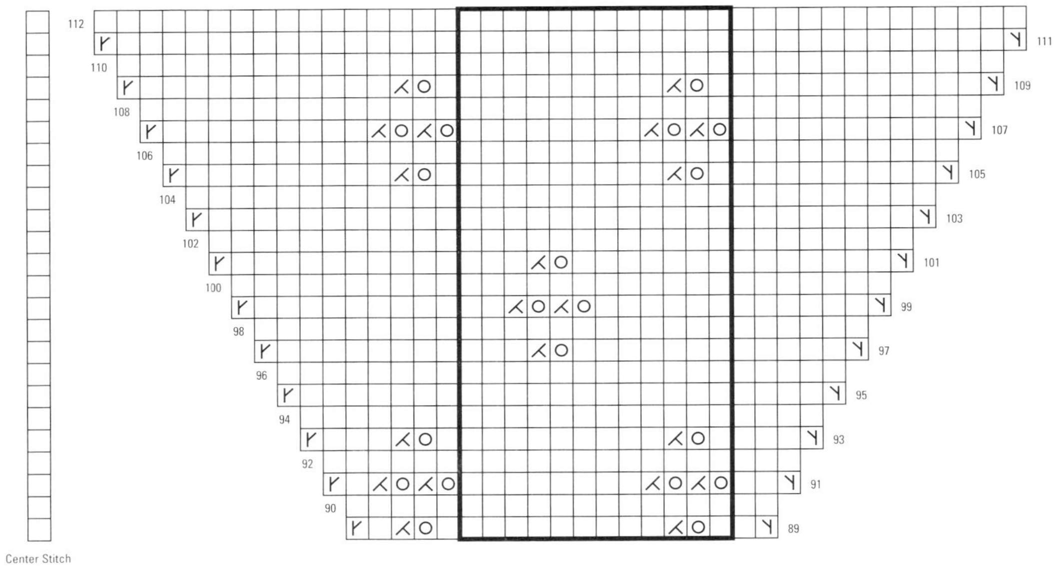

Center Stitch

Chart 5: *Foreground Flowers*

Work boxed area 4 times total

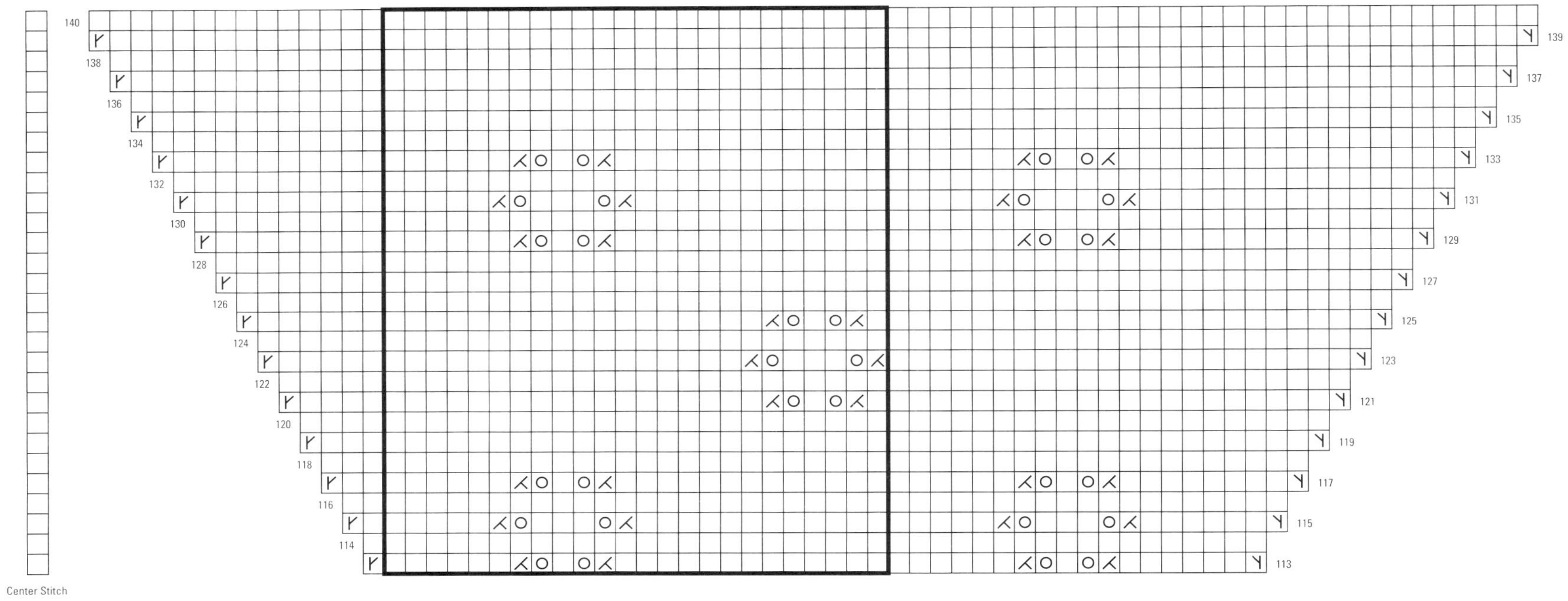

Center Stitch

Left Side of Chart 6: *Lake of Shining Waters*　　Work boxed area 5 times total

Center Stitch

Right Side of Chart 6: *Lake of Shining Waters*　　Work boxed area 5 times total

Motoring Madness

Wind In The Willows
Kenneth Grahame
1908

"Certainly not!" replied Toad emphatically. "On the contrary, I faithfully promise that the first motor-car I see, poop-poop! off I go in it!" *Chapter VI: Mr. Toad*

Finished Measurements
6"/ 15cm from cuff to tip;
7½"/ 19cm circumference

Yarn
The Fiber Company *Acadia*; 145yds/ 133m per 1.75oz/ 50g; 60% Merino Wool, 20% Baby Alpaca, 20% Silk; dk weight: 1 skein in *Amber*
OR
approx 145yds/ 133m of a dk weight yarn

Needles/Notions
Size 2 US/ 2.75mm circular needle, 12"/ 30cm or preferred small circular method
Size 3 US/ 3.25mm circular needle, 12"/ 30cm or preferred small circular method
Size 3 US/ 3.25mm set of five double-point needles
Change needle size if needed in order to obtain the correct gauge
Cable needle, 2 stitch holders, 2 stitch markers

Gauge
22sts/ 32rows = 4x4"/ 10x10cm in Stockinette Stitch with larger needles

Mr. Toad of Toad Hall is a compulsive creature. Whenever he starts a hobby, he throws himself into it so deeply that little else exists in his world. No expense is too great, either. Rat and Otter have seen Toad go from interest to interest. But nothing could have prepared them for Toad's obsession with motor-cars.

Despite being in love with driving, it turns out that Toad is a poor driver. He drives fast and swerves all over the road. Smashing car after car, Toad continues to buy big, expensive motor-cars, which Grahame likely based on early models of the Rolls Royce. Toad's compulsion goes so far that, passing by and seeing an unattended motor-car, he decides to see how easily it starts. One thing leads to another, and soon Toad lands in jail for grand theft auto.

Left Mitt

With smaller circular needles, CO 40 sts. Place marker and join in round, taking care not to twist the stitches.

Ribbing Set Up: [P1, k1 tbl] 17 times, p2, [p1, k1 tbl] 2 times.
Continue in pattern until work measures 1"/ 2.5cm from CO edge.

Switch to larger circular needles.

Next Rnd: K20, pm, work row 1 of Left Chart: *Toad On The Loose.*
Next Rnd: Knit to marker, sm, work next row of *Left Chart: Toad On The Loose.*
Continue in pattern until row 8 of Left Chart: *Toad On The Loose* has been completed.

Begin Thumb Gusset
Rnd 9: Knit to marker, sm, m1L, pm, work row 9 of Left Chart: *Toad On The Loose.*
Rnd 10: Knit to marker, sm, knit to marker, sm, work next row of Left Chart: *Toad On The Loose.*

Rnd 11: Knit to marker, sm, m1L, knit to marker, m1R, sm, work next row of Left Chart: *Toad On The Loose.*
Repeat rounds 10 and 11 six more times, then round 10 once more. Row 24 of Left Chart: *Toad On The Loose* will have been completed. There will be 15 thumb stitches between the markers.

Separate Thumb
Rnd 25: Knit to marker, remove the marker, slip the next 15 sts onto the stitch holder, sm, work next row of Left Chart: *Toad On The Loose.*

Rnds 26-36: Knit to marker, sm, work next row of Left Chart: *Toad On The Loose.*
Switch to smaller needles.

Ribbing Set Up: [p1, k1 tbl] 16 times, p2, [p1, k1 tbl] 3 times.
Continue in pattern until ribbing measures 1"/ 2.5cm.

BO loosely in established ribbing pattern. Use a knit stitch rather than k1 tbl while binding off.
Put in the thumb.

Thumb – Use For Both Mitts

Place the 15 sts from the holder evenly onto dpns. Pick up one stitch in the gap between the first and last stitch from the holder. This picked-up stitch will be the last stitch in the round.
Rnd 1: Knit. 16 sts.
Ribbing Set Up
Next Rnd: [p1, k1 tbl]
Continue in pattern until ribbing measures 1"/ 2.5cm.
BO loosely in established ribbing pattern. Use a knit stitch rather than k1 tbl while binding off.

Right Mitt

With smaller circular needles, CO 40 sts. Place marker and join in round, taking care not to twist the stitches.

Ribbing Set Up: [K1 tbl, p1] 2 times, p2, [k1 tbl, p1] 17 times.
Continue in pattern until work measures 1"/ 2.5cm from CO edge.

Switch to larger circular needles.

Next Rnd: Work row 1 of Right Chart: *Drivers Beware*, pm, k20.
Next Rnd: Work next row of Right Chart: *Drivers Beware*, sm, knit to end.
Continue in pattern until row 8 of Right Chart: *Drivers Beware* has been completed.

Begin Thumb Gusset
Rnd 9: Work row 9 of Right Chart: *Drivers Beware*, sm, m1L, pm, knit to end.
Rnd 10: Work next row of Right Chart: *Drivers Beware*, sm, knit to marker, sm, knit to end.
Rnd 11: Work next rnd of Right Chart: *Drivers Beware*, sm, m1L, knit to marker, m1R, sm, knit to end.
Repeat rounds 10 and 11 six more times, then round 10 once more. Row 24 of Right Chart: *Drivers Beware* will have been completed. There will be 15 thumb stitches between the markers.

Separate Thumb
Rnd 25: Work row 25 of Right Chart: *Drivers Beware*, remove marker, slip the next 15 sts onto the stitch holder, sm, knit to end.
Rnds 26-36: Work next row of Right Chart: *Drivers Beware*, sm, knit to end.

Switch to smaller needles.

Ribbing Set Up: [K1 tbl, p1] 3 times, p2, [k1 tbl, p1] 16 times.
Continue in pattern until ribbing measures 1"/ 2.5cm.

BO loosely in established ribbing pattern. Use a knit stitch rather than k1 tbl while binding off. Put in the thumb.

Weave in all the ends and block both mitts.

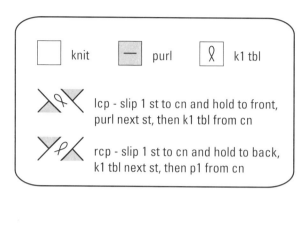

| | knit | ▭ | purl | ℓ | k1 tbl |

lcp - slip 1 st to cn and hold to front, purl next st, then k1 tbl from cn

rcp - slip 1 st to cn and hold to back, k1 tbl next st, then p1 from cn

Left Chart: *Toad On The Loose*

Right Chart: *Drivers Beware*

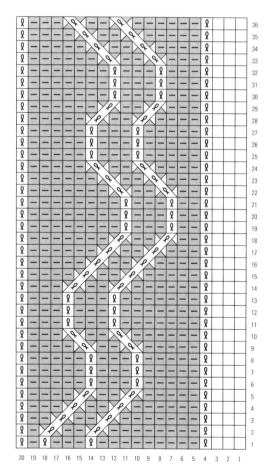

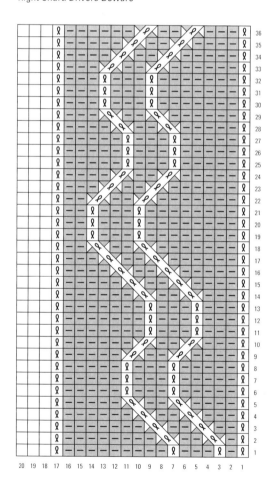

Behind The Garden Wall

The Secret Garden
Frances Hodgson Burnett
1911

"Perhaps it has been buried for ten years," she said in a whisper. "Perhaps it is the key to the garden!"

Chapter VII: The Key To The Garden

Finished Measurements
Small (Large);
8"/ 20cm (9"/ 23cm) around calf and ball of foot unstretched;
9"/ 23cm (9"/ 23cm) from cuff to heel

Yarn
Ella Rae *Lace Merino*; 460yds/ 420m per 3.5oz/ 100g skein; 100% Extra Fine Merino Wool; fingering weight:
1 (1) skein in #16 *Forest Green* (MC)
1 (1) skein in #23 *Faded Green* (CC)
OR
approx 290 (330)yds/ 265 (302)m (MC), 200 (220)yds/ 183 (201)m (CC) of a fingering weight yarn

Needles/Notions
Size 0 US/ 2.0mm circular needle, 12"/ 30cm or preferred small circular method
Size 1 US/ 2.25mm circular needle, 12"/ 30cm or preferred small circular method
Size 1 US/ 2.25mm set of five double-point needles
Change needle size if needed in order to obtain the correct gauge
Stitch holder, 4 stitch markers

Gauge
32sts/ 40rows = 4x4"/ 10x10cm in Stockinette Stitch with larger needles
For the most accurate gauge, knit the swatch using the first 32 stitches of the first chart

After her parents die, sickly Mary Lennox moves from India to her uncle's residence, Misselthwaite Manor in England. Soon after her arrival, Mary learns that somewhere on the estate, there is a hidden garden behind a locked gate. And the only key that could unlock the gate was buried long ago.

Despite the existence of many walled gardens, it doesn't take Mary long to find a walled garden with no entrance. There are tree tops poking above the wall, but try as she might, she cannot locate the door. Ivy chokes the walls, even though it is the dead of winter. Ivy is a hardy, evergreen plant, and without someone maintaining it, the vines can quickly overtake walls and gardens. So Mary spends her time looking for the secret door and the hidden key, all the while regaining her health and strength.

Notes

The color is worked with the stranded method. See the stranded color tutorial on pg 87 for additional help.

Cuff

With smaller circular needle, CO 64 (72) sts in MC. Place marker and join in round, taking care not to twist the stitches.

Cuff Set Up: [K2, p2]
Continue in pattern until work measures 2"/5cm from CO edge.

Leg

Switch to larger needle.
Next 2 Rnds: Knit

Size Small ONLY
Work Chart 1 Small: *Hunt For The Door.*

Size Large ONLY
Work Chart 1 Large: *Hunt For The Door.*

Heel

The first 32 (36) sts will become the heel.

Size Small ONLY
Knit the first 32 sts in the established striped pattern.

Size Large ONLY
Knit the first 35 sts in the established striped pattern. Knit the 36th stitch in the MC.

All Sizes
Slip the remaining 32 (36) sts onto the stitch holder. Turn work.
Row 1 (WS): Slip first stitch as if to purl. Purl across in the established striped pattern.
Turn work.
Row 2 (RS): Slip first stitch as if to purl. Knit across in the established striped pattern.
Repeat rows 1 and 2 until heel is 2½ (2¾)"/6.5 (7)cm long or desired length. End on a WS row.

Turn The Heel

Keep in striped pattern.

Size Small ONLY
Set Up Row (RS): K20 in established stripe pattern, skp.
Turn work.
Row 1 (WS): Sl 1, p9, p2tog
Turn work.
Row 2 (RS): Sl 1, k9, skp
Turn work.
Repeat rows 1 and 2 until all stitches have been worked, ending on a RS. Do not turn work. 11 sts.

Size Large ONLY
Set Up Row (RS): K22 in established stripe pattern, skp.
Turn work.
Row 1 (WS): Sl 1, p9, p2tog
Turn Work.
Row 2 (RS): Sl 1, k9, skp
Turn Work.
Repeat rows 1 and 2 until all stitches have been worked, ending on a RS. Do not turn work. 11 sts.

Shape Gusset

Only one sock should have the key on the bottom. Be sure to make one sock following the Plain Foot instructions and one sock following the Key Foot instructions.

Plain Foot

Keeping in striped pattern, pick up and knit each of the slipped stitches along the heel flap plus an additional stitch between the heel flap and top of the foot, pm. This marker is now the beginning of the round.
Set up rnd: Work row 1 of Chart 2 Small: *Ivy Trail* (Chart 2 Large: *Ivy Trail*), pm. Keeping in striped pattern, pick up and knit one stitch between the top of the foot and the heel flap, then pick up and knit each slipped stitch along the heel flap. *Be sure that the striped pattern matches the heel.* Count backwards from the stripes on the heel in order to line up the stripes correctly. Knit to end.

Rnd 1: Knit next row of Chart 2 Small: *Ivy Trail* (Chart 2 Large: *Ivy Trail*), sm, skp, knit until 2 sts from next marker, k2tog.
Rnd 2: Knit next row of Chart 2 Small: *Ivy Trail* (Chart 2 Large: *Ivy Trail*), sm, knit to end.

Repeat rnds 1 and 2 until there are 65 (73) sts total. End on rnd 2.

Next Rnd: Knit next row of Chart 2 Small: *Ivy Trail* (Chart 2 Large: *Ivy Trail*), sm, skp, knit to end. 64 (72) sts.

Continue working Chart 2 Small: *Ivy Trail* (Chart 2 Large: *Ivy Trail*) until the chart has been completed.

Key Foot

Keeping striped pattern, pick up and knit each of the slipped stitches along the heel flap plus an additional stitch between the heel flap and top of the foot, pm. This marker is now the beginning of the round.
Set up rnd: Work row 1 of Chart 2 Small: *Ivy Trail* (Chart 2 Large: *Ivy Trail*), pm. Keeping in striped pattern, pick up and knit one stitch between the top of the foot and the heel flap, then pick up and knit each slipped stitch along the heel flap. *Be sure that the striped pattern matches the heel.* Count backwards from the stripes on the heel in order to line up the stripes correctly. Pm, work row 1 of Chart 3: *Buried Key*, pm, knit to end.

Rnd 1: Work next row of Chart 2 Small: *Ivy Trail* (Chart 2 Large: *Ivy Trail*), sm, skp, knit to marker, sm, work next row of Chart 3: *Buried Key*, sm, work in pattern until 2 sts before the end of the rnd, k2tog.
Rnd 2: Work next row of Chart 2 Small: *Ivy Trail* (Chart 2 Large: *Ivy Trail*), sm, knit to next marker, sm, work next row of Chart 3: *Buried Key*, sm, knit to end.

Repeat rnds 1 and 2 until there are 65 (73) sts total. End on rnd 2.

Next Rnd: Knit next row of Chart 2 Small: *Ivy Trail* (Chart 2 Large: *Ivy Trail*), sm, skp, knit to marker, knit next row of Chart 3: *Buried Key*, sm, knit to end. 64 (72) sts.

Continue working Chart 2 Small: *Ivy Trail* (Chart 2 Large: *Ivy Trail*), and Chart 3: *Buried Key* until the charts have been completed. Once the Chart 3: *Buried Key* has been completed, the stitch markers on either side of it can be removed.

Foot

Continue knitting in the established striped pattern until the sock is 2"/ 5cm from desired length.

Toe

Switch to dpns as needed when working toe.

Size Small ONLY
Work Chart 4 Small: *Garden's Edge*.

Size Large ONLY
Work Chart 4 Large: *Garden's Edge*.

Once the chart has been completed, slip the first 12 (16) sts onto one dpn. Slip the remaining 12 (16) sts onto a second dpn. Use the MC to graft the toe together.

Weave in all ends and block both socks.

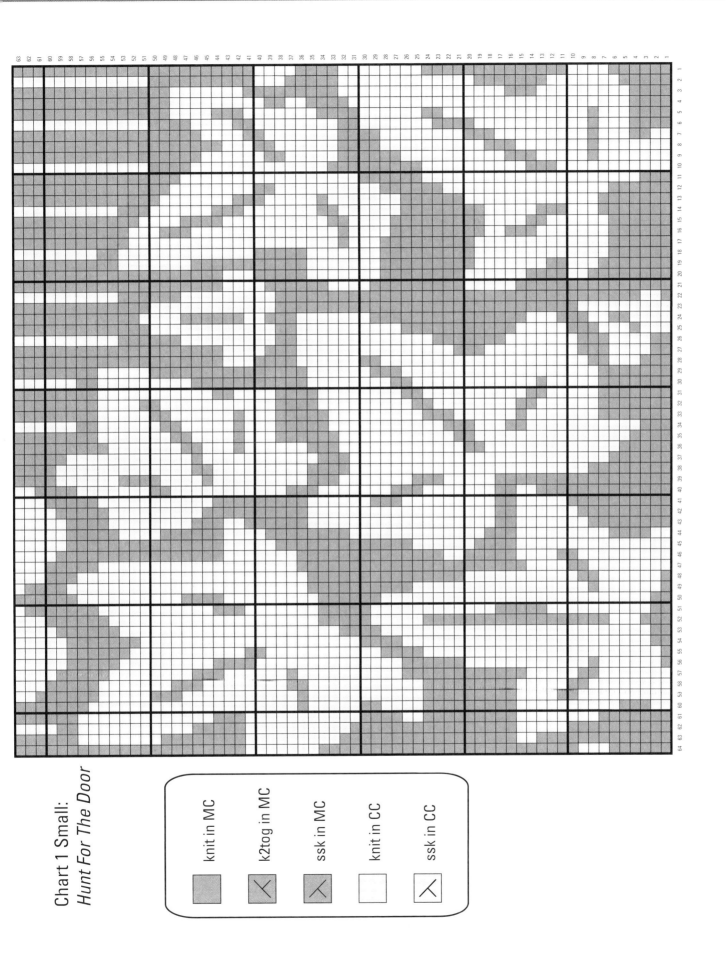

Chart 1 Small:
Hunt For The Door

knit in MC

k2tog in MC

ssk in MC

knit in CC

ssk in CC

Chart 1 Large: *Hunt For The Door*

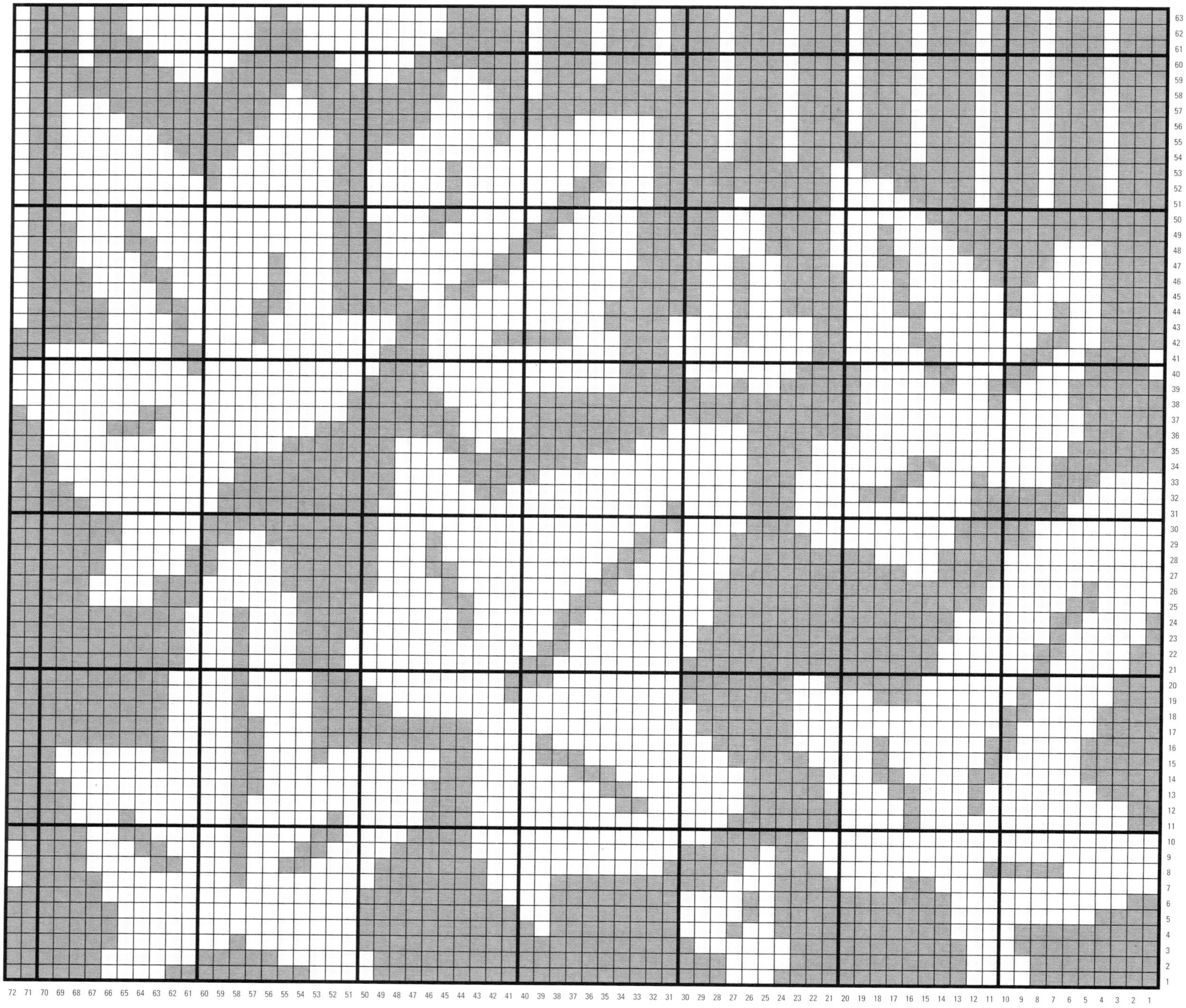

▨	knit in MC
⟋ (boxed)	k2tog in MC
⟍ (boxed)	ssk in MC
☐	knit in CC
⟍	ssk in CC

Chart 2 Small: *Ivy Trail*

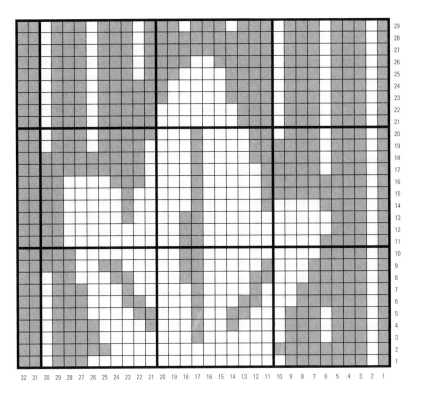

Chart 2 Large: *Ivy Trail*

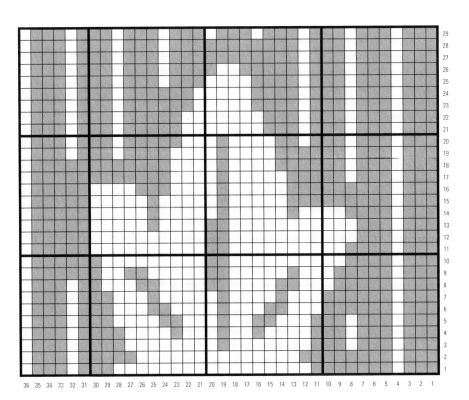

Chart 3: *Buried Key*

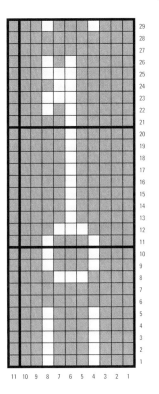

Chart 4 Small: *Garden's Edge*

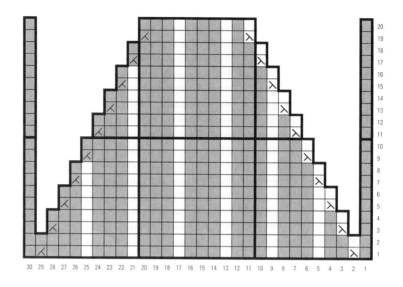

Chart 4 Large: *Garden's Edge*

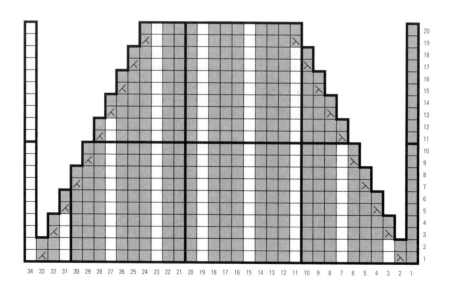

Abbreviations

"	Inch
BO	Bind off
c2b	Cable 2 back. Sl 1 st to cn, hold to back, k1, then k1 from cn
c2f	Cable 2 front. Sl 1 st to cn, hold to front, k1, then k1 from cn
c3bk2tog	Cable 3 back, k2tog. Sl 2 sts to cn, hold to back, k1, then knit the two stitches on the cn together
c3b	Cable 3 back. Sl 1 st to cn, hold to back, k2, then k1 from cn
c3f	Cable 3 front. (RS) Sl 2 sts to cn, hold to front, k1, then k2 from cn (WS) Sl 1 st onto cn, hold to front, p2, then p1 from cn
c4b	Cable 4 back. Sl 2 sts to cn, hold to back, k2, then k2 from cn
c4f	Cable 4 front. Sl 2 sts to cn, hold to front, k2, then k2 from cn
CC	Contrast color
cm	Centimeter
cn	Cable needle
CO	Cast on
dpn(s)	Double point needle(s)
g	Gram
lcp	Left cross purl. Slip 1 st to cn and hold to front, purl next st, then k1 tbl from cn
k1 tbl	Knit one through back loop
k2tog	Knit two together; right leaning decrease
k	Knit
kfb	Knit in the front and back of the stitch; see pg 91
m1L	Make one left; see pg 91
m1R	Make one right; see pg 91
m1P	Make one purl; see pg 91
m	Meter
MC	Main color
mm	Millimeter
oz	Ounce
p2tog	Purl two together; right leaning decrease
p	Purl
pm	Place marker
psso	Pass slipped stitch over
rcp	Right cross purl. Slip 1 st to cn and hold to back, k1 tbl next st, then p1 from cn
rnd(s)	Round(s)
RS	Right side
s2kp2	Slip two stitches, knit the next stitch, pass the two slipped stitches over the knitted stitch; center double decrease
skp	Slip the first stitch, knit the next stitch, pass the slipped stitch over the knitted stitch; left leaning decrease
sl	Slip stitch; unless otherwise noted, slip the stitch as if to purl
sm	Slip marker
ssk	Slip, slip, knit; left leaning decrease
st(s)	Stitch(es)
t2b	Twist 2 back. Sl 1 st to cn, hold to back, k1, then p1 from cn
t2f	Twist 2 front. Sl 1 st to cn, hold to front, p1, then k1 from cn
t3b	Twist 3 back. Sl 1 st to cn, hold to back, k2, then p1 from cn
t3f	Twist 3 front. (RS) Sl 2 sts to cn, hold to front, p1, then k2 from cn (WS) Sl 1 st to cn, hold to front, p2, then k1 from cn
t4b	Twist 4 back. Sl 2 sts to cable needle, hold to back, k2, then p2 from cn
t4f	Twist 4 front. (RS) Sl 2 sts to cn, hold to front, p2, then k2 from cn (WS) Sl 2 sts to cn, hold to front, p2, then k2 from cn
WS	Wrong side
w&t	Wrap and turn; see pg 93
yd(s)	Yard(s)
yo	Yarn over

Techniques

Backwards Loop Cast On

1. Create a backwards loop and place on the needle. (Fig. 1)

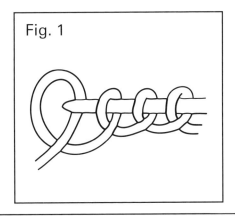

Fig. 1

Provisional Cast On

1. With a crochet hook and waste yarn, chain stitch a few more stitches than cast on stitches needed. (Fig. 1)
2. Turn the chain over so that the back bumps of the chain are facing upwards. Insert a knitting needle through the back bump. (Fig. 2)
3. Pull the yarn through. (Fig. 3)
4. Repeat steps 2 and 3 until the number of stitches that are needed have been reached. (Fig. 4)

When the stitches are ready to be worked, pull out the end of the chain stitch to unzip the waste yarn and reveal the live stitches.

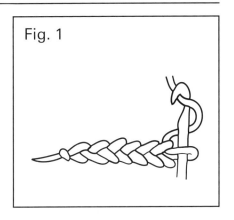

Fig. 1

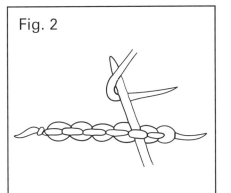

Fig. 2

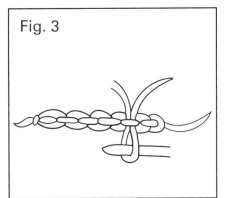

Fig. 3

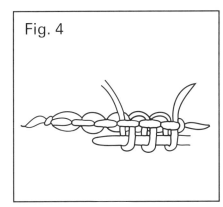

Fig. 4

Tab Cast On

1. Cast on 3 stitches. Knit 6 rows. Do not turn work after knitting the last row.
2. Rotate the piece 90 degrees counterclockwise and pick up three stitches. (The stitches are along the garter stitch ridge.) (Fig. 1)
3. Rotate the piece 90 degrees again. Pick up and knit 3 sts on the end of the tab. (Fig. 2)
9 sts total.

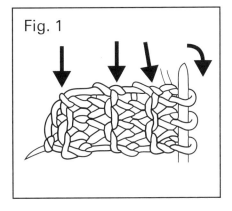

Fig. 1

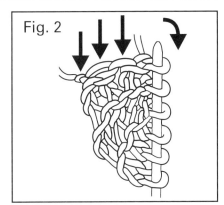

Fig. 2

Circular Cast On

1. Arrange the yarn in a clockwise manner, loop the yarn so that the yarn end is crossed over the top of the working end. (Fig. 1)

2. Pull the yarn end under the ring. This loop is where the needle will slip through. (Fig. 2)

3. With the needle pointing above the ring, pull the working end of the yarn over the top of the needle, then below the underside of the ring. (Fig. 3)

4. With the needle pointing into the center of the ring, pull the working yarn over the top of the needle, then back upwards underneath the ring. (Fig. 4)

5. Continue steps 3 and 4 until the number of stitches needed has been reached. (Fig. 5) Due to the nature of this cast on, an odd number of stitches always has to be cast on at first. If an even number of cast on stitches is needed, cast on one extra. It will be slipped off the needle during step 7.

6. Divide the stitches evenly onto three needles. Do not turn. The first round will begin with the first stitch that was cast on. (Fig. 6)

7. Knit the first round. For a cast on needing an even number of stitches, slip the extra stitch off of the needle when you reach it. Once several rounds have been knit, the loose end of the yarn can be pulled to close the hole. (Fig. 7)

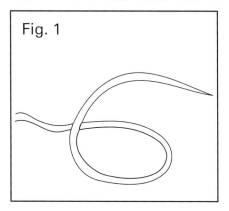

Fig. 1

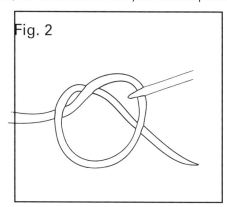

Fig. 2

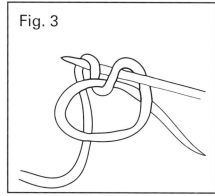

Fig. 3

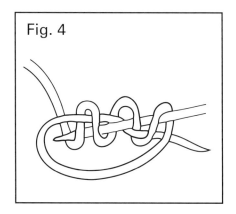

Fig. 4

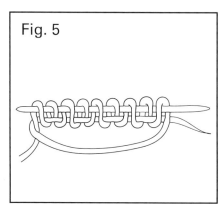

Fig. 5

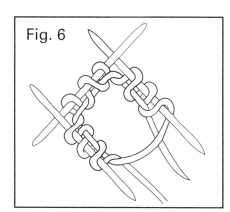

Fig. 6

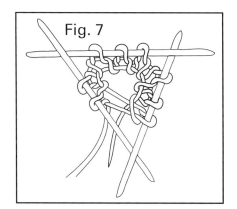

Fig. 7

Intarsia

1. When switching colors on the knit-side of the work, wrap the color to be worked around the *back* of the color already worked before continuing on. (Fig. 1)
2. When switching colors on the purl-side of the work, wrap the color to be worked around the *front* of the color already worked before continuing on. (Fig. 2)

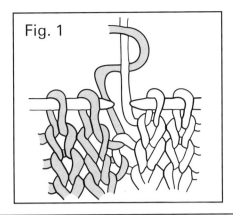

Fig. 1

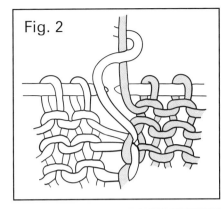

Fig. 2

Stranded Color - Wrapping CC Strands

Note: Typically wraps are made after every four to five stitches.

1. Have the CC crossed behind the MC. (Fig. 1)
2. Wrap the MC counterclockwise around the CC. (Fig. 2)
3. Knit the stitch with the MC. The long CC float has now been wrapped.

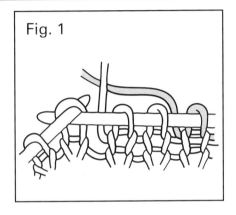

Fig. 1

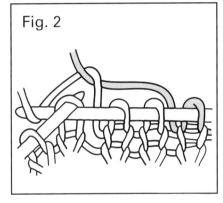

Fig. 2

Stranded Color - Wrapping MC Strands

1. Wrap the MC around the right needle as if to knit. Wrap the CC around the right needle as if to knit. Be sure that the CC is on the leftmost part of the right needle. (Fig. 3)
2. Unwrap the MC from the right needle. (Fig. 4)
3. Knit the stitch with the CC. The long MC float has now been wrapped.

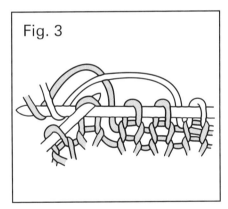

Fig. 3

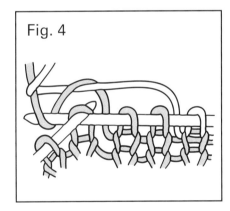

Fig. 4

k1 tbl

1. Insert the right needle purlwise into the back of the next stitch. (Fig. 1)
2. Knit the stitch.

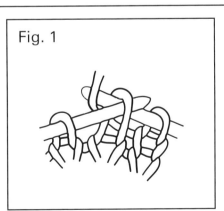

Fig. 1

Grafting - Stockinette

Set Up - These two steps are only done once when beginning to graft.

1. Thread the tapestry needle purlwise through the first stitch on the front knitting needle. (Fig. 1) Leave the stitch on the needle.
2. Thread the tapestry needle knitwise through the first stitch on the back knitting needle. (Fig. 2) Leave the stitch on the needle.

Repeated Steps

3. Thread the needle knitwise through the first stitch on the front needle. (Fig. 3) Slip the stitch off of the needle.
4. Thread the needle purlwise through the next stitch on the front needle. (Fig. 4) Leave the stitch on the needle.
5. Thread the needle purlwise through the first stitch on the back needle. (Fig. 5) Slip the stitch off of the needle.
6. Thread the needle knitwise through the next stitch on the back needle. (Fig. 6) Leave the stitch on the needle.
7. Continue working steps 3-6 until all the stitches have been worked. When there is only one stitch left on the front and back needle, work the front stitch as in (Fig. 3) and the back stitch as in (Fig. 5).

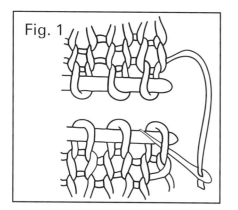

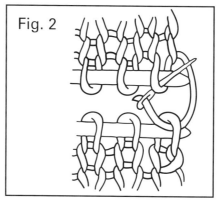

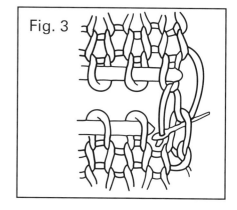

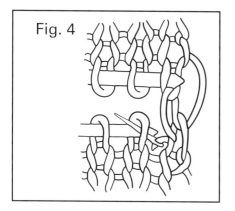

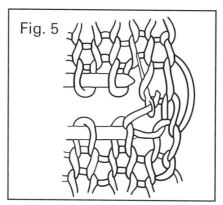

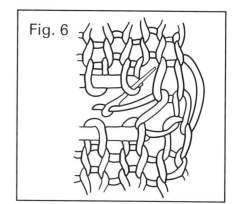

Grafting - Reverse Stockinette

When grafting reverse stockinette stitches together, the steps are the same as grafting stockinette stitches, but all the steps done on the front needle are done to the back needle and all the steps done on the back needle are instead done on the front needle.

Set Up - These two steps are only done once when beginning to graft.
1. Thread the tapestry needle knitwise through the first stitch on the front knitting needle. (Fig. 1) Leave the stitch on the needle.
2. Thread the tapestry needle purlwise through the first stitch on the back knitting needle. (Fig. 2) Leave the stitch on the needle.
Repeated Steps
3. Thread the needle purlwise through the first stitch on the front needle. (Fig. 3) Slip the stitch off of the needle.
4. Thread the needle knitwise through the next stitch on the front needle. (Fig. 4) Leave the stitch on the needle.
5. Thread the needle knitwise through the first stitch on the back needle. (Fig. 5) Slip the stitch off of the needle.
6. Thread the needle purlwise through the next stitch on the back needle. (Fig. 6) Leave the stitch on the needle.
7. Continue working steps 3-6 until all the stitches have been worked. When there is only one stitch left on the front and back needle, work the front stitch as in (Fig. 3) and the back stitch as in (Fig. 5).

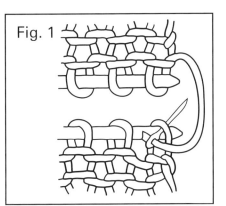

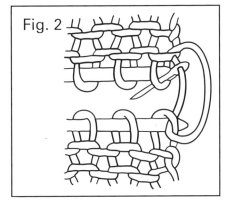

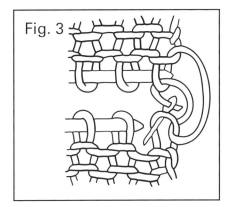

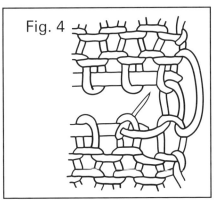

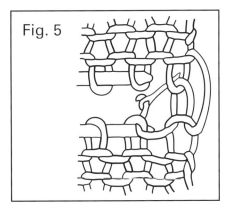

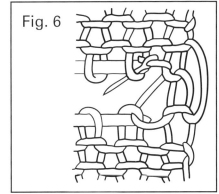

Grafting from Knit to Purl

When switching from knit to purl stitches while grafting, the front needle is worked the same as if both stitches were knit stitches. There is a different procedure for the back needle.

1. Thread the needle knitwise through the first stitch on the front needle. (Grafting - Stockinette Fig. 3) Slip the stitch off of the needle.
2. Thread the needle purlwise through the next stitch on the front needle. (Grafting - Stockinette Fig. 4) Leave the stitch on the needle.
3. Thread the needle purlwise through the first stitch on the back needle. (Fig. 7) Slip the stitch off of the needle.
4. Thread the needle purlwise through the next stitch on the back needle. (Fig. 8) Leave the stitch on the needle.

Continue on by using the instructions from Grafting - Reverse Stockinette.

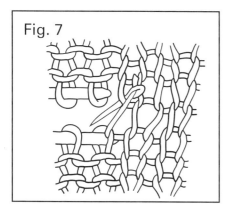

Fig. 7

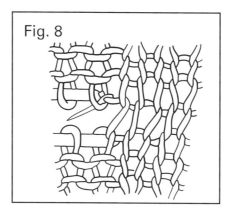

Fig. 8

Grafting from Purl to Knit

When switching from purl to knit stitches while grafting, the front needle is worked the same as if both stitches were purl stitches. There is a different procedure for the back needle.

1. Thread the needle purlwise through the first stitch on the front needle. (Grafting - Reverse Stockinette step 3) Slip the stitch off of the needle.
2. Thread the needle knitwise through the next stitch on the front needle. (Grafting - Reverse Stockinette step 4) Leave the stitch on the needle.
3. Thread the needle knitwise through the first stitch on the back needle. (Fig. 9) Slip the stitch off of the needle.
4. Thread the needle knitwise through the next stitch on the back needle. (Fig. 10) Leave the stitch on the needle.

Continue on by using the instructions from Grafting - Stockinette.

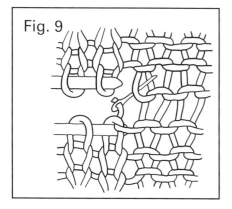

Fig. 9

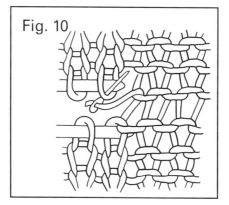

Fig. 10

kfb - Knit in the front and back

1. Knit into the stitch to be increased. Do not slide the stitch off of the left needle. (Fig. 1)
2. Insert right needle into the back of the working stitch and knit through the back loop. (Fig. 2)

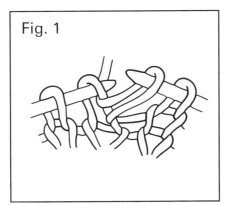

Fig. 1

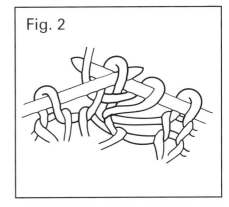

Fig. 2

m1L - make one left

1. With the left needle, from front to back, lift the strand that appears between the just-worked stitch and the next stitch. (Fig. 1)
2. Knit the stitch through the back loop. (Fig. 2)

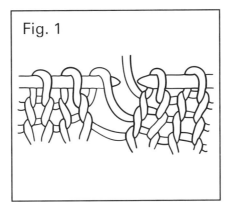

Fig. 1

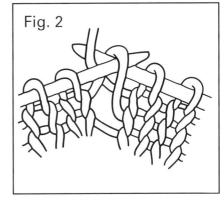

Fig. 2

m1R - make one right

1. With the left needle, from back to front, lift the strand that appears between the just-worked stitch and the next stitch. (Fig. 1)
2. Knit the stitch through the front loop. (Fig. 2)

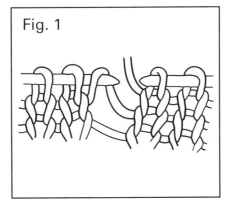

Fig. 1

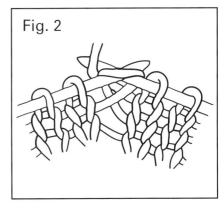

Fig. 2

m1P   make one purl

1. With the left needle, from back to front, lift the strand that appears between the just-worked stitch and the next stitch. (Fig. 1)
2. Purl the stitch through the back loop. (Fig. 2)

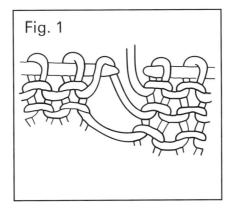

Fig. 1

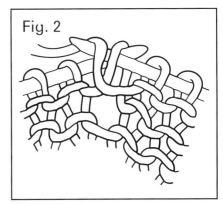

Fig. 2

Pom-Pom

1. Trace a copy of the Pom-Pom Template onto a piece of cardstock. Cut it out.
2. Wrap yarn around the template. (Fig. 1) The more densely the yarn is wrapped, the thicker the pom-pom will be.
3. Thread yarn through all the wrapped yarn. Pull the yarn so that it is near the center of the ring. (Fig. 2)
4. Tie a knot in the threaded yarn. Do not pull the knot tight. Cut the wrapped yarn along the outer edge of the template. (Fig. 3)
5. Once all the yarn has been cut, pull the knot tight. Add an extra knot or two to secure the yarn.

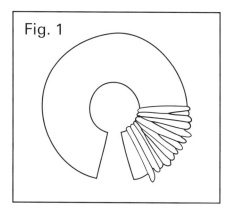

Fig. 1

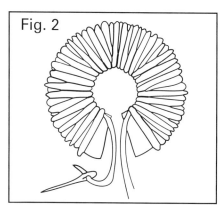

Fig. 2

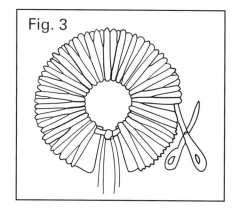

Fig. 3

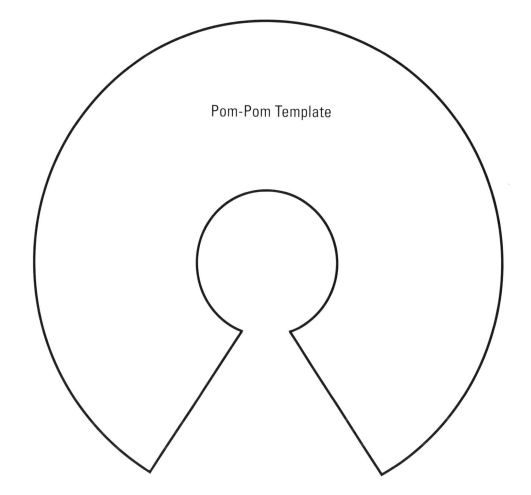

Pom-Pom Template

Short Rows - w&t on the RS

1. With yarn in front, slip the next stitch from the left needle to the right, purlwise. (Fig. 1)
2. With yarn in back, slip the unknit stitch on the right needle back to the left needle. (Fig. 2)
3. Turn the work, continue on in pattern.

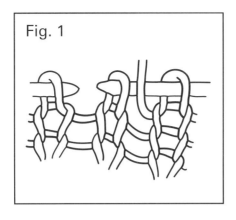

Fig. 1

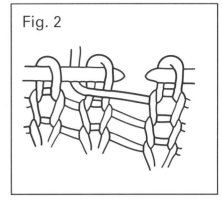

Fig. 2

Short Rows - w&t on the WS

1. With yarn in back, slip the next stitch from the left needle to the right, purlwise. (Fig. 3)
2. With yarn in front, slip the unknit stitch on the right needle back to the left needle. (Fig. 4)
3. Turn the work, continue on in pattern.

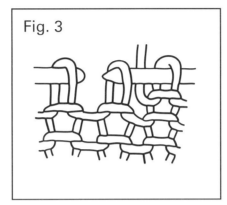

Fig. 3

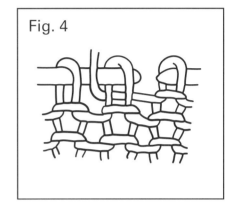

Fig. 4

Short Rows - Picking Up Wraps on the RS

1. With the right needle, lift the front of the wrap up and over the wrapped stitch. (Fig. 5) The wrap should be behind the now-unwrapped stitch. If there is more than one wrap, pull all the wraps over the stitch.
2. Knit both stitches together through the back loop. (Fig. 6) If there is more than one wrap, knit all the stitches together through the back loop.

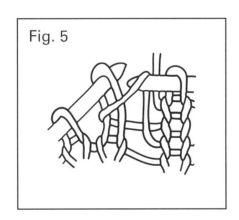

Fig. 5

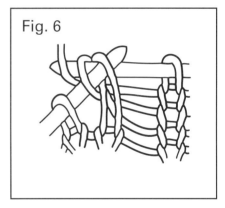

Fig. 6

Short Rows - Picking Up Wraps on the WS

1. With the right needle, lift the back of the wrap up and over the wrapped stitch. (Fig. 7) The wrap should be in front of the now-unwrapped stitch. If there is more than one wrap, pull all the wraps over the stitch.
2. Purl both stitches together. (Fig. 8) If there is more than one wrap, purl all the stitches together.

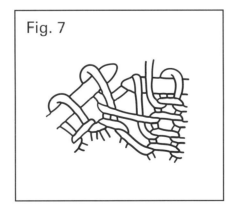

Fig. 7

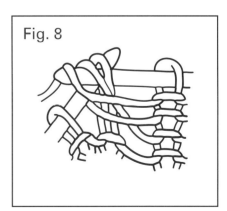

Fig. 8

Acknowledgments

It takes a village to write a book. If I had known how hard it was going to be, I might have never started. Luckily, I had an enormous "village" who helped me along the way.

To my parents, I'm sorry. I know I was difficult to live with while working on this. Thanks for putting up with me, defending me when people asked why I wasn't getting a "real job", and believing in me long before I believed in myself. Mum, I still can't believe you drove six hours round trip plus two hours of photographing just so "Brinker" could have snow in the background. Dad, I can't believe you let us do it.

Thanks to my Oma, who has been an inspiration. I wouldn't have even started knitting without seeing your work. Thanks also to all my relatives who cheered me on and helped me out, even when I didn't know I needed it.

To my models: Elaine F., Karl M., Christopher N., Janna O., Kris R., Jacqueline R., Jim R., Alina S., Matt S., & Travis S. You guys were all rockstars. I don't think the weather was ever pleasant for any shoot. It was either absurdly hot or wickedly cold. Thanks for sticking it out and looking like you were having a great time. These projects look so much better because of you guys.

Thanks to all my lighting assistants: Vanessa L., Karl M., Juliet N., Peter N., Jacqueline R., Jim R., & Alina S. I'm sure you didn't know what you were getting yourselves into, but I couldn't have gotten such great images without you.

To my test knitters: Cathy, Christine, Cindy, David, Debbie, Kerry, Lilly, Margaret, Melissa, Nicci, Rachael, Sandra, Stephanie, Tyler, and Wei Siew: Thanks for spending your time knitting all these projects. Your suggestions have made these patterns so much easier to understand. And I appreciate that none of you guys made me feel like a weenie when there was a problem.

Thank you Chris for tech editing and Alina for copyediting. You sussed out all sorts of errors that I would have never found. Thanks to you I feel confident putting these patterns out into the world.

Thank you to all my blog buddies who, without even seeing one design, said that they would be interested in buying this book. Ivy, Wei Siew, and Andi, you guys in particular gave me the confidence to continue on through some very bleak-looking days.

To Rich and Marci, the "Deep Sea Wanderer" and "Black Beauty Rides On" photo shoots would not have happened without your help. Thanks for all the ego boosts and enthusiasm.

Thanks to Jim and Jackie, who let me crash on their couch. So much of this book wouldn't have been possible without your support. You guys are awesome.

To my Green Planet Yarn family: it has been a pleasure working with all of you. Extra thanks to Beth for supporting my patterns and running an excellent yarn shop.

A big thanks to Paty for providing props, helping me name charts, and checking up on me.

A shout-out to Navreet for helping choose the final images. I don't think you ever thought you'd be making judgment calls on knitting photos.

Thanks to A.J., Justin, Mick, and everyone else who endured my "I'm feeling sad" phone calls. You guys deserve a medal of some sort.

Thanks to everyone who was a part of this process. Even if you weren't specifically named, there is a good chance I was about to quit when you took time to help me out.

Thanks to you, my readers, who have bought this book. You now own a little piece of my dream. I hope that these projects bring a little bit of light into your world.

And Scooter. You spent so many afternoons sitting next to me, waiting for your walk. Thanks for the patience and company, little buddy. Now let's go for your walkies!

Timeline

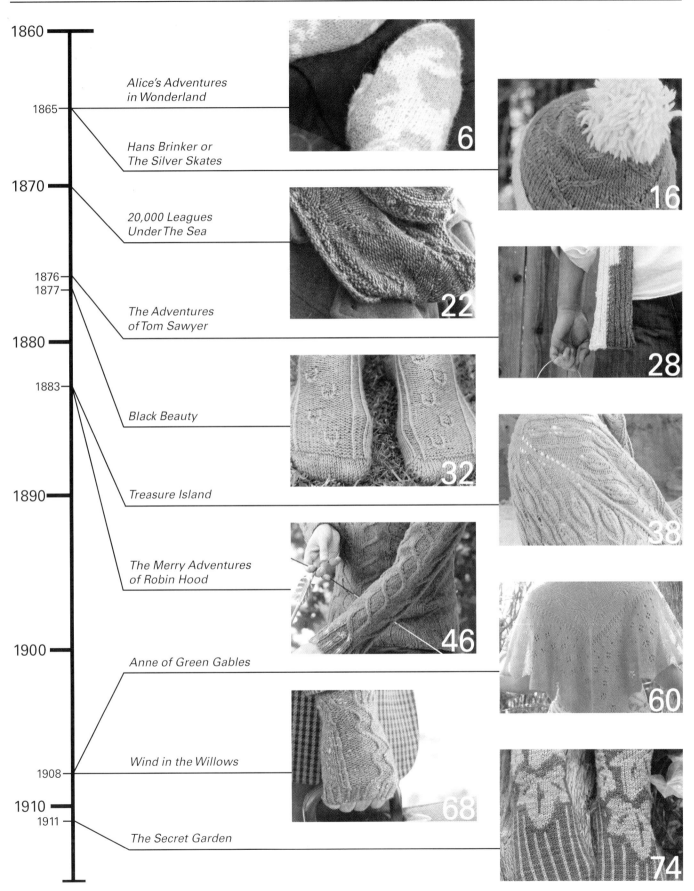

1860

1865 — Alice's Adventures
in Wonderland — **6**

Hans Brinker or
The Silver Skates — **16**

1870

20,000 Leagues
Under The Sea — **22**

1876
1877

The Adventures
of Tom Sawyer — **28**

1880

1883

Black Beauty — **32**

1890

Treasure Island — **38**

The Merry Adventures
of Robin Hood — **46**

1900

Anne of Green Gables — **60**

Wind in the Willows — **68**

1908

1910
1911

The Secret Garden — **74**